I0202813

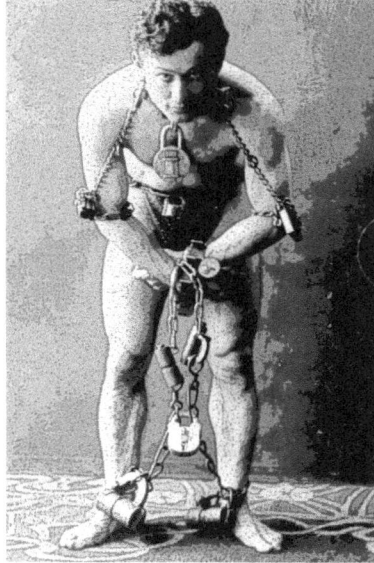

BOOKS BY TROY TAYLOR

DEAD MEN SO TELL TALES SERIES
Dead Men Do Tell Tales (2008)
Bloody Chicago (2006)
Bloody Illinois (2008)
Bloody Hollywood (2008)
Without a Trace (2009)

HAUNTED ILLINOIS BOOKS
Haunted Illinois (1999 / 2001 / 2004)
Haunted Decatur (1995 / 2009)
More Haunted Decatur (1996)
Ghosts of Millikin (1996 / 2001)
Where the Dead Walk (1997 / 2002)
Dark Harvest (1997)
Haunted Decatur Revisited (2000)
Flickering Images (2001)
Haunted Decatur: 13th Anniversary (2006)
Haunted Alton (2000 / 2003 / 2008)
Haunted Chicago (2003)
The Haunted President (2005 / 2009)
Mysterious Illinois (2005)
Resurrection Mary (2007)
The Possessed (2007)
Weird Chicago (2008)

HAUNTED FIELD GUIDE BOOKS
The Ghost Hunters Guidebook
(1997/ 1999 / 2001/ 2004 / 2007)
Confessions of a Ghost Hunter (2002)
Field Guide to Haunted Graveyards (2003)
Ghosts on Film (2005)
So, There I Was (with Len Adams) (2006)
Talking with the Dead (with Rob & Anne Wlodarski)
(2009)

HISTORY & HAUNTINGS SERIES
The Haunting of America (2001)
Into the Shadows (2002)
Down in the Darkness (2003)
Out Past the Campfire Light (2004)
Ghosts by Gaslight (2007)

OTHER GHOSTLY TITLES
Spirits of the Civil War (1999)
Season of the Witch (1999/ 2002)
Haunted New Orleans (2000)
Beyond the Grave (2001)
No Rest for the Wicked (2001)
Haunted St. Louis (2002)
The Devil Came to St. Louis (2006)
Sex & the Supernatural (2009)
Houdini: Among the Spirits (2009)

STERLING PUBLICATIONS
Weird U.S. (Co-Author) (2004)
Weird Illinois (2005)
Weird Virginia (Co-Author) (2007)
Weird Indiana (Co-Author) (2008)

BARNES & NOBLE PRESS TITLES
Haunting of America (2006)
Spirits of the Civil War (2007)
Into the Shadows (2007)

HISTORY PRESS TITLES
Wicked Washington (2007)

STACKPOLE BOOKS TITLES
Haunted Illinois (2008)
True Crime Illinois (2009)
Big Book of Illinois Ghost Stories (2009)

HOUDINI

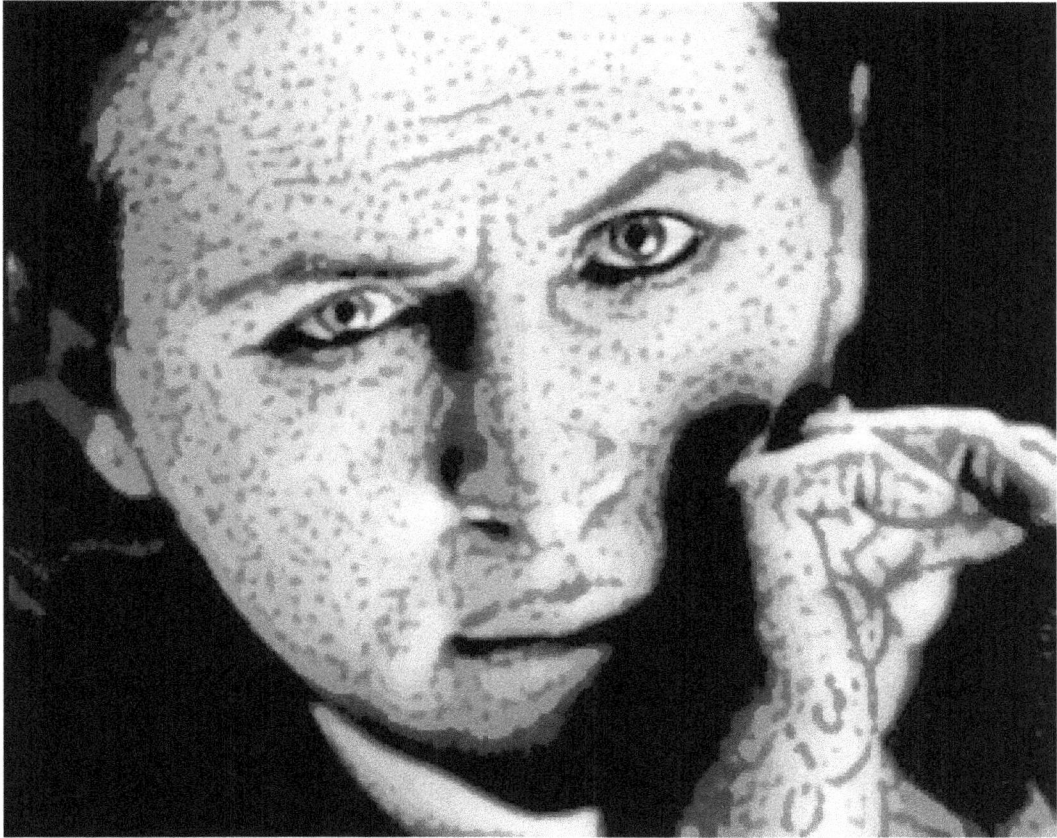

AMONG THE SPIRITS
BY TROY TAYLOR

- A Dark Haven Entertainment Book from Whitechapel Press -

This book is for all of the kind readers and attentive audiences, who read what I wrote about Spiritualism and listened to me talk about its strange history and never complained -- even though they would have rather been reading, or listening to me talk about, other things!

Thanks to Rene & Elyse for their friendship, support and encouragement.

And to Haven -- who brought magic into my life.

© COPYRIGHT 2009 BY TROY TAYLOR
AND DARK HAVEN ENTERTAINMENT, INC.

All Rights Reserved, including the right to copy or reproduce this book, or portions thereof, in any form, without express permission from the author and publisher

ORIGINAL COVER ARTWORK DESIGNED BY

©Copyright 2009 by Michael Schwab & Troy Taylor

Visit M & S Graphics at http: www.manyhorses.com/msgraphics.htm

THIS BOOK IS PUBLISHED BY:

Whitechapel Press

A Division of Dark Haven Entertainment, Inc.

Chicago, Illinois / 1-888-GHOSTLY

Visit us on the internet at http://www. American Hauntings .org

First Printing -- October 2009

ISBN: 1-892523-68-X

Printed in the United States of America

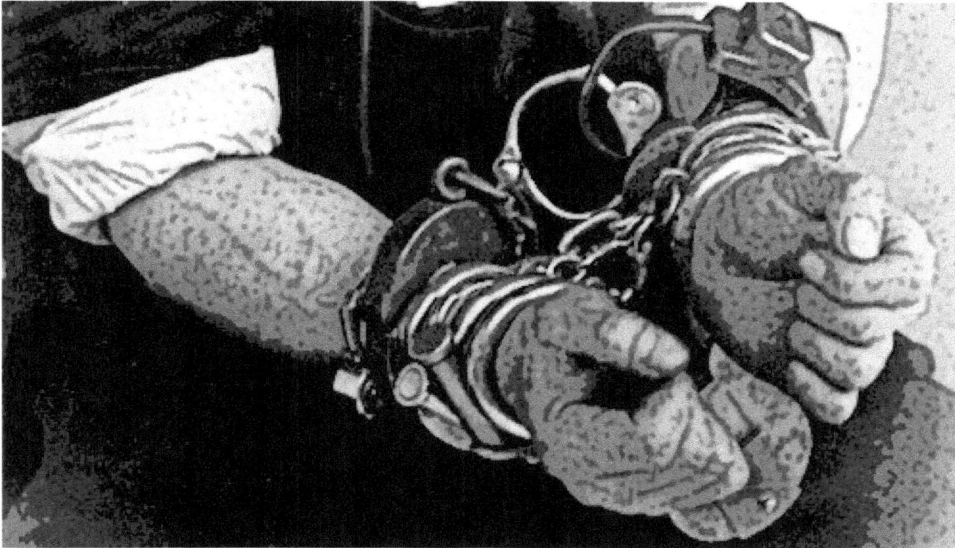

Nothing I ever read concerning the so-called Spiritualistic phenomenon has impressed me as being genuine. It is true that some of the things I read seemed mystifying but I question if they would be were they reproduced under different circumstances, under test conditions, and before expert mystifies and opened-minded committees. Mine has not been an investigation of a few days or weeks or months but one that has extended over thirty years and in that thirty years I have not found one incident that savored of the genuine.

Harry Houdini

He had the essential masculine quality of courage to a supreme degree. Nobody has ever done and nobody in all human probability will ever do such reckless feats of daring. His whole life was one long succession of them.

Sir Arthur Conan Doyle

My chief task has been to conquer fear. The public sees only the thrill of the accomplished trick; they have no conception of the tortuous preliminary self-training that was necessary to conquer fear no one except myself can appreciate how I have to work at this job every single day, never letting up for a moment. I always have on my mind the thought that next year I must do something greater, something more wonderful.

Harry Houdini

HOUDINI: AMONG THE SPIRITS

INTRODUCTION: THE TEST

The dim light cast eerie shadows on the faces of the three men who stood in the drawing room. One of them, the owner of the home in which the test was going to take place, poured brandy into a small, cut crystal glass. The man, Bernard Ernst, the respected president of the American Society of Magicians, swallowed the amber liquor and turned to face his two friends. They were very different men, both in looks and stature, and were violently opposed to the other's spiritual philosophies. They had once been close friends, but their differences had driven them apart. Ernst had managed to bring the two of them together on this night, hoping once and for all to convince one of the men that his belief about the talents of the other were completely unfounded.

Ernst smoothed his thick dark beard and turned to the taller of the two men. Sir Arthur Conan Doyle, the eminent author turned Spiritualism proponent. Even though he was considerably older than the others, he gave the robust appearance of a man of much younger years. He accepted Ernst's offer of a glass of brandy and raised it to his lips, which were barely visible under his luxuriant white mustache.

Doyle was one of the most famous men in the world. He had been a writer for decades, creating one of the most beloved characters in history, the famous detective Sherlock Holmes. In recent years, though, Doyle had turned his back on most of his paid work and had devoted his time to lecturing and writing about Spiritualism, a religious faith that promoted the idea that it was possible to make contact with the dead. It had been Spiritualism that had destroyed the friendship between Doyle and the third man in the room.

This man, a small, wiry fellow with dark, unruly hair, stood a few steps away from the others. He declined his own snifter of brandy, intent on the task that was before him. In just moments, he planned to prove to his former friend that his seemingly magical gifts were not supernatural in origin -- they were merely illusion, learned by years of mastering the skills of deception. The man's name was Harry Houdini and, like Conan Doyle, he was one of the most well-known men in the world.

Doyle and Houdini had once been very good friends. It was a friendship built on their shared interest in the unknown. Doyle's belief in the supernatural was

Houdini and Conan Doyle in better times at the height of their friendship

unshakeable, while Houdini wanted to believe, but found nothing in which he could put his faith. Eventually, he became jaded with the antics of fake Spiritualists and his once open mind slowly began to close. The two friends had many arguments about the reality of the paranormal. The arguments were long and inconclusive, but good-natured. Neither convinced the other to his respective point of view but both of them found their own interest stirred by their friendship. They met when possible and wrote scores of long and fascinating letters.

They formed a close bond but it would be a series of strange events over the next two years that would bring this unusual friendship to an end. The rift began when Doyle started to publicly take the side of Spiritualists who believed that Houdini accomplished some of his greatest magic using supernatural powers. Houdini had long been working to expose fraudulent mediums in private, in print and during his stage shows, which made him a much-hated figure in Spiritualist circles. Some believed they had an explanation for this --- they stated that Houdini's exposure of mediums was a deliberate ploy to cover the fact that he was a medium himself! They claimed that many of his extraordinary escapes were accomplished by Houdini "dematerializing" from the traps in which he had placed himself. "This ability," Doyle stated publicly, "to unbolt locked doors is undoubtedly due to Houdini's mediumistic powers and not to any normal operation of the lock. The effort necessary to shoot a bolt from within a lock is drawn from Houdini the medium, but it must not be thought that this is the only means by which he can escape from his prison. For at times, his body can be... dematerialized and withdrawn."

This placed Houdini in the classic magician's dilemma, meaning that he could only go so far in denying the Spiritualist claims. He could state that his escapes were simple trickery, but little else. By saying any more, he would have to expose how his escapes were accomplished, which he could never do, not if he wished to keep drawing audiences. His escapes were managed by purely physical means, he said. His crusade against Spiritualism was simply a way to protect the general public from charlatans. As for himself, Houdini claimed to keep an open mind on the subject and did not assume that all mediums were frauds.

Spiritualist leaders declared that Houdini's actions did not agree with his words and so the magician made a pact with a number of friends. The pact promised that whichever of them died first would make every attempt to contact the others by way of a secret code. But Houdini still could not escape the claims being made by Doyle, so he devised a plan to make the author realize that all of his tricks were just that --- tricks. He assured Doyle that he would give him proof that magic was accomplished through simple trickery.

Bernard Ernst agreed to arrange a meeting between Doyle and Houdini at his home. Houdini had explained to him that he was going to arrange a special illusion for Doyle so that he could show the man that he was not a psychic medium and that skill alone was responsible for his amazing tricks. The three men had dinner together, the coolness between Doyle and Houdini never quite thawing, and then they adjourned to the drawing room. Once in the room, Houdini began preparing for his illusion. He opened a wooden case and took out a number of items that he would use.

Using a wire, Houdini suspended an ordinary slate in the center of the room. It was attached to an overhead fixture and placed in a position that made it obvious that it could not be manipulated by anything else in the room. Houdini invited Doyle to examine the slate and then he handed the author five plain balls that were made from cork. Doyle rolled the balls around in his large hand and examined them closely. He juggled them back and forth in his hands, weighing each of them and trying to see if one might be heavier than the others. Finally, satisfied that each of the balls was exactly alike, he chose one of them at random. At Houdini's direction, he dropped it into small container of white paint. With a forefinger, he pushed it down into the paint, allowing the cork to soak up the thick liquid.

Next, Houdini handed him a piece of paper and a pencil. "Please write down any words of phrase that you would like, Sir Arthur, but please do not let me see what you have written," Houdini instructed him. "You are welcome to leave the room, or even the house if you like, to ensure that your message remains a secret."

Paper in hand, Doyle walked out of the drawing room. He exited the house, walked three blocks and turned a corner. He shielded the paper with his hand, looked all around him to make sure that no one could see him, and wrote down a short message. When he finished writing, Conan Doyle folded the paper carefully and placed it in his pocket. He looked around once more and, satisfied that the nearby streets were empty, he returned to the Ernst home.

While Doyle had been away, Ernst stayed in the drawing room with Houdini, ensuring that the magician had remained in the room the entire time. Houdini had sat silently in a chair, with his eyes closed and his fingers folded together. He appeared to be completely at peace. He only stirred when Doyle walked back into the room.

As the author waited with anticipation, Houdini asked him to carefully remove the paint-soaked cork ball from the can of paint and stick it to the face of the slate, which was still suspended in the air. Doyle plucked the now white ball out of the paint and gently pressed it to the slate. It stuck to the surface as if it were affixed with adhesive. Ernst passed him a handkerchief and he wiped the residue of paint from his fingers. As he stood there watching, Houdini made a few theatrical flourishes and the cork ball inexplicably began to roll over the surface of the slate. As it rolled, words began to form behind it, spelling out the biblical phrase, Mene Mene Tekel Upharsin. The words, from the Book of Daniel, are often referred to as "the writing on the wall."

Doyle was visibly startled by this turn of events -- they were the exact words that he had written on the piece of paper! How could such an amazing feat have been accomplished? This could be nothing more than the work of the supernatural. If it wasn't, then how could Houdini have done it?

The illusionist refused to tell how he had managed the trick. How could he? It was a cardinal rule among practitioners of magic that the secrets of illusions could never be revealed. But he assured Conan Doyle that it was only a trick, nothing more. He had certainly not used any occult powers to make the cork ball move or to spell out the phrase that Doyle had secretly written on the paper. The author demanded to know though, if he had not used mysterious powers, then how had he managed to cause the events to happen. Houdini would not tell him.

Bernard Ernst, a magician himself, even joined in with his own plea. He begged Houdini to explain how the trick worked, either to himself or Doyle, in the strictest confidence, but Houdini refused. Strangely, he would never use the trick again in any of his shows and no one has ever been able to reproduce it. At that time, Bernard Ernst admitted that the trick reminded him of a certain mind-reading stunt that Houdini had stopped using because, as he explained to Ernst, it was "too spooky."

So, how was it done? To this day, no one knows. Houdini always maintained that the illusion was nothing more than simple trickery but Doyle was more convinced than ever of Houdini's supernatural powers.

There is no question that Houdini spent the majority of his life immersed in the trappings of the occult, both as an investigator and debunker. He is also considered one of the greatest illusionists and magicians in history. Many of his stunts and escapes were so fantastic that those who witnessed them refused to believe that he carried them out by normal means. They claimed that his debunking of fraudulent mediums was only done to cover up for the fact that he was a talented medium himself. What is likely closer to the truth was that Houdini only attacked fake mediums out of frustration and anger over the fact that they were not the real thing. It was not that he did not believe in the supernatural, he was more than willing to accept the possibility of its existence. He began going to Spiritualists in an attempt to try and contact his dead mother, but found that the mediums he met were often frauds. This was when he turned to exposing them, still searching for the truth. Before his death, Houdini stated that should it be possible to contact the living from the other side, he would do so.

The question remains as to whether or not he succeeded.

THE YOUNG MAGICIAN

Harry Houdini was born Erik Weisz in Budapest, Hungary, on March 24, 1874 but grew up as Erich Weiss in the small Wisconsin town of Appleton. Later, his father, Rabbi Mayer Samuel Weiss, moved the family to Milwaukee and he took over a Reform Jewish congregation there. Legend has it that young Erich was apprenticed to a locksmith, where he learned to assemble and take apart locks with his eyes closed. If this part of the story is true, it was a skill that served him well later in life. Many aspects of Houdini's life remain a mystery today (which is likely how he wanted it) and he has been credited with the famous line about his biography: "When the legend is greater than the truth -- print the legend!"

At the age of twelve, Erich ran away from home, hoping to contribute more to his impoverished parents than he could make shining shoes and selling newspapers. Rabbi Weiss left for New York a short time later, feeling that a teacher of religion could do better in a city with a larger Jewish population. Erich worked his way east and joined his father. Between the two of them, they saved enough money to bring Erich's mother and the other six children to Manhattan.

Magic was one of Erich's many interests until he read the memoirs of the famous French magician, Jean Eugene Robert-Houdin. Erich was working at a necktie factory on lower Broadway but more than anything he wanted to become a professional magician. He left his first steady job and, assisted by his friend and fellow factory worker Jacob Hyman, he began appearing in New York beer halls and theaters. He took the name of Houdini, which was based on the name of Robert-Houdin, and he and Hyman broke in their new act playing one-night stands wherever they could find a booking. Discouraged when agents refused to book them for longer runs, Hyman quit and went back to the necktie factory. Theodore Weiss, Erich's young brother, eagerly took his place. Performing for the most part in dime museums, on platforms next to snake charmers, fire-eaters and human oddities, they traveled as far west as Chicago, where the "Brothers Houdini" did quite well during the 1893 World's Columbian Exposition, performing twenty shows daily for $18 a week on the Midway. While not actually inside the fair, the Midway Plaisance, as it was grandly called, was close enough to the action to draw large crowds, many of whom came to gawk at "Little Egypt," the first belly dancer to perform on American soil. The Houdini brothers wore dark face makeup and flowing robes and, chanting a jumble of nonsense syllables, passed themselves off as conjurers from the mysterious East.

Friends knew Houdini as "Ehrie," so the Americanization of his first name to "Harry" was almost inevitable. To his parents, though, he was always Erich. Before Rabbi Weiss died at the age of sixty-three, he called his son to his bedside and made Erich swear that he would always provide for his mother. This vow was unnecessary. Cecilia had made the costumes for Erich's first magic act and had encouraged him in his career. Erich loved his mother deeply and the bond between them grew stronger (some would say almost unnaturally so) with the passage of years.

Houdini continued to travel and perform, mostly in dime museums throughout the Midwest. Dime museums were the lowest rung on the ladder of theatrical entertainment. The salaries they offered were small, but they gave up-and-coming performers the chance to polish their acts. There were seldom fewer than six shows a day and sometimes, on weekends and holidays, as many as twenty. The first proprietors of dime museums had relied on works of art and natural wonders to lure in the public. By the 1890s, magicians, sword swallowers, fire-eaters and human oddities had become major attractions.

A young Erich Weiss in his teens. He was still working as a necktie cutter when this photograph was taken.

At one show in Milwaukee, Houdini struck up a conversation with a bearded German named Dr. Josef Gregorowich and got his first taste of Spiritualism. Gregorowich, who introduced himself as a spiritual healer and hypnotist, invited Houdini to a séance that he was holding at a private home in the city. Houdini was more than happy to accept and that night, he watched as the German stood by the bedside of a sick woman. He held an empty glass over his head and called for the lights to be turned out. As the room was plunged into semi-darkness, Gregorowich pleaded for healthy energy from the spirit world. When the gaslights were ignited again, he claimed that the glass was now filled with "spirit medicine."

Houdini was so intrigued that his new friend offered to show him other "wonders." He jotted down his address and gave it to Houdini. The magician later wrote, "I thought surely a man who lived so close to the police station must be honest."

At Gregorowich's suggestion, Houdini inspected an upright wooden post that had been nailed to the floor in the bedroom. A metal ring was bolted to the center of it. The German sat on a stool in front of the column as Houdini then tied the man's hands behind his back with a surgical bandage and knotted it a dozen times. He then tied the ends of the strip to the metal ring in the post. He tied the medium's neck at the back in a similar fashion, and nailed the ends of the cloth to the top of the post. He used two more strips to secure the medium's legs to the legs of the stool. Finally, each knot was sewn with a needle and thread and wound up with adhesive tape. An ordinary spoon was placed in a coffee cup on Gregorowich's lap, far out of reach of his hands or his mouth.

Gregorowich nodded toward the curtained doorway between the bedroom and a sitting room. He told Houdini to step into the parlor, close the curtain, and ask any questions that came to mind. He told him, "The spirits will answer with one clang for yes, two for no." Houdini followed his directions and as soon as he proposed a question, the spoon, behind the curtain, banged out a reply in the coffee cup.

Houdini pulled aside the drapes. He found Gregorowich tied exactly as he had been when the curtain was closed. Houdini was stunned. He knew that wrists could be bound for a quick release -- he had done it himself -- but he knew that the German could not have used this technique to free his hands. The young magician was impressed by the trick, if it was a trick, and for many years he wondered how it had been accomplished. He later found the secret of the trick in an old book. It was devilishly ingenious. He had been looking for a cleverly hidden release, when one wasn't needed. By sliding his seated body back and to the left of the post and straining to bring his tied hands forward, the performer could reach the spoon. The book, called *The Bottom Facts Concerning the Science of Spiritualism*, explained that a series of knots, tied one atop the other, plus the diameter of the metal ring to which the ends of the strip were tied, allowed just enough leeway for one hand to produce spirit "manifestations."

It was Houdini's first encounter with a phony medium, but it would not be the last.

Erich's brother, Theo, affectionately known as "Dash", replaced Joe Hyman in the magic act and went on tour with his brother

After the Columbian Exposition in Chicago, the Houdini brothers returned to New York. They played for a week at Miner's Bowery over the Fourth of July 1894, while other, more popular acts were entertaining crowds at the seashore. Later that summer, their dime museum bookings in Manhattan ranged from the Harlem Museum to Worth's midtown showplace, where they were held over for a three-week run. At Worth's, they started a new feature to the act. Houdini was padlocked in an empty beer barrel, from which he managed to escape in less than twenty seconds. One of the brothers' most applauded illusions continued to be one that they called "Metamorphosis," which involved an assistant who was placed into a locked box and then switched places with the magician within seconds after a curtain was raised. Theo, whom Houdini called "Dash," could make the switch very quickly but Houdini's wife, Bess, was even faster.

Houdini met Wilhelmina Beatrice Rahner while he was performing at Coney Island. There are three different versions of the couple's whirlwind courtship. Bess said that she was in the front row when Houdini gave a school show in Brooklyn. He accidentally knocked a glass from his table and stained her dress. Her mother was furious and threatened to have the apologetic young magician arrested. Bess managed to whisper to Harry that she thought he was wonderful. Mrs. Rahner, sensing trouble, halted her tirade and stalked away with her daughter in tow. Harry csaid he first met Bess on a streetcar. He was on his way to give a show for a private party and when he dropped his equipment, a pretty young woman in a white dress helped him to pick it up. To his surprise, she turned out to be a guest at the birthday party where he was performing. It was at the party where Harry remembered ruining the girl's dress. He arranged for his mother to make a new dress for the girl, which he delivered to Brooklyn. Bess recalled slipping out of the house and going to Coney Island with Harry, where they spent the evening together. At the end of the night, Bess said that she didn't want to go home and so when Harry proposed to her, she accepted. They bought rings and were married by midnight. In Harry's version of the story, he remembered the proposal, but not at Coney Island. Bess was wearing her new dress when they passed City Hall and as a wedding party was coming out, she remarked that she looked like a bride in her white dress and Harry, a bridegroom. Impulsively, Harry suggested that they get married, and they did.

The third and most likely version of the story was offered by Theo, Harry's brother. Bess, he said, was one half of a song-and-dance act called The Floral Sisters. He

Houdini and Bess as a young married couple

Houdini with his wife and mother -- his "two sweethearts", as he wrote on the photograph.
Bess knew to never come between her husband and his mother, although Cecilia loved her daughter-in-law very much.

introduced Bess to Harry and the two fell in love. Two weeks later, they disappeared and returned as man and wife. Harry was only twenty years old and Bess was eighteen. She weighed only ninety-four pounds and was even shorter than Houdini's diminutive height, which biographers say was no more than five feet, five inches. No matter how the two of them met, every version of the story agreed on the reaction of the couple's parents. Mrs. Rahner flew into a rage and refused to speak to Houdini. She couldn't understand how her Catholic daughter could marry the son of a rabbi. She continued to shun Bess for twelve years after the marriage until 1906, when Harry and one of his brothers went to her home and refused to leave until she agreed to visit Bess, who was seriously ill. Cecilia Weiss was very understanding, though, and welcomed the newlyweds into her home. Following their civil ceremony, Harry and Bess, to please their parents, repeated their marriage vows in separate ceremonies with a priest and a rabbi. Bess said soon after, "I'm the most married person I know, three times -- and to the same man."

Bess began working with her husband and Theo went on the road with another girl, "Madame Olga," as his assistant. Bess was able to change places with Houdini during the "Metamorphosis" illusion at a speed that Theo readily admitted was beyond his power.

In October, the Houdinis played for two weeks at Barton's Theater in Newport News, Virginia, and three months later they were booked at Tony Pastor's Theater in New York. Pastor's intimate show house was in the Tammany Building on East 14th Street and was a prime spot for a new act to be seen. But if Harry thought this was to be his entry into the big time, he was disappointed. There was no invitation for a return engagement.

Tony Pastor scrawled his opinion of the show on a sheet of theater stationary dated February 4, 1895: "The Houdinis act as performed here I found satisfactory and interesting." It was a single sentence that, for a sensitive performer struggling to make a name for himself, chilled the heart.

HOUDINI THE SPIRIT MEDIUM

Harry and Bess played for twenty-six weeks in 1895 with the Welsh Brothers Circus, which maintained winter headquarters in Lancaster, Pennsylvania. When not performing magic, Harry sold soap, combs, toothpaste and other necessities to his fellow performers. During his act, he manipulated playing cards, changed the color of silk handkerchiefs, yanked knotted pieces of braid through his neck, and shot a borrowed watch to the center of a target. Bess sang and danced and together, they presented a second-sight act. Harry, as he walked through the audience, cued the blindfolded Bess with code words that allowed her to identify various objects that spectators removed from their pockets and handbags. They always used "Metamorphosis," their most applauded feat, to close the act.

In Harry's spare time, he pursued his new hobby --- tinkering with handcuffs. Handcuffs were seldom used by magicians when Harry acquired his first pair. He discovered that they could be opened with a concealed duplicate key, a small piece of metal or a bent wire. A single key would open every set of the same pattern. With less than a dozen hidden keys and picks, Houdini was sure that he could escape from every kind of manacle used by various police departments in the United States. He read every piece of information that he could find on locking mechanisms and began collecting different kinds of cuffs, taking them apart and studying their mechanisms.

Houdini began employing a variety of new and strange stunts in his act and devised incredible escapes that had never been attempted before. He became known for some time as the "Handcuff King," due to the ease from which he escaped any restraints. It was a skill that would later make him famous.

Though Houdini sent half of his weekly $20 salary home to his mother, by the end of the tour with Welsh Brothers, he had saved enough to buy an interest in The American Gaiety Girls, a burlesque show. His cousin, Harry Newman, was the company's advance man, traveling ahead of the production, booking theaters and raising publicity. The investment seemed wise. The

Harry and Bess toured with the Welsh Brothers Circus in 1895. The Houdinia are in the front row, to the right, just to the left of the clown in the striped suit.

Houdinis would be working regularly and Houdini could display his new escape skills to get free newspaper space for the shows.

In November 1895, Houdini amazed officers at a police station in Gloucester, Massachusetts, by freeing himself from a pair of their handcuffs. Similar stories began to appear in newspapers wherever the show went. Houdini was gaining a good reputation and he and Bess seemed to be well on their way to success. But it was not meant to be, at least not yet. The show closed abruptly in Rhode Island when the company manager was arrested for embezzlement.

Disappointed, Houdini signed on with Marco the Magician to tour Nova Scotia. Marco had hoped to emulate Herrmann the Great but business was so bad in Halifax that he gave up the show and returned to Connecticut, where he was a church organist.

Houdini stayed on in Canada, hoping to make it on his own. He was playing in St. John, the principal city of New Brunswick, when he accompanied a recent doctor friend on his rounds in a mental institution. Houdini watched in shocked fascination as a man in a straitjacket, locked in a padded cell, tried frantically to free himself. Houdini became convinced that an escape from a straitjacket would be an effective one to perform on stage. He obtained a straightjacket from his friend and then, after weeks of strenuous practice, was ready to try it before an audience. Eager volunteers buckled Houdini in, carried him to a cabinet and then closed the curtains. He had gained some slack by holding his crossed arms rigidly as the sleeve straps were fastened.

Harry began perfecting his straitjacket escape, long before it became one of the most sensational parts of his act.

Straining every muscle, a little at a time, he forced one sleeve and then other over his head. Then, he opened the straps with the pressure of his fingers through the canvas. He twisted, turned, and finally squirmed free. He threw off the restraint and burst through the curtains to take a bow.

No one applauded. The escape had fallen flat because the audience had not witnessed his struggle. They assumed that a hidden assistant had released him. Houdini had not yet discovered the showmanship that would allow him to hold an audience enthralled.

The Houdinis had their worst winter season so far in 1896 and new bookings eluded them until the spring. In August, they were in so much trouble financially that Harry wrote to magicians Harry Kellar and Herrmann the Great and offered the services of he and Bess as assistants. Kellar wrote back to say that he wasn't hiring at this time but offered Houdini luck in the future. He never received a reply from Herrmann the Great.

In the fall of 1897, Houdini toured with Dr. Hill's California Concert Company, a Midwestern medicine show. The regular salary from Hill, $25 a week, offered the Houdinis a small amount of security. Dr. Hill, the owner, sold bottled cure-alls to crowds that gathered in small towns to watch the free entertainment supplied by members of his troupe. He then sold tickets for another show to be performed later on in the evening.

The show was a hodgepodge of singers, dancers, comedians and a melodrama called "Ten Nights in a Barroom," above the evils of alcohol. The Houdinis presented their magic and escapes, Bess sang, and together, they doubled as actors in the play.

In one town, Dr. Hill heard that a professional spirit medium had been attracting sizable audiences and Houdini offered to stage a séance as part of their performance. Eager to see his name at the top of the handbill, he promised Dr. Hill that he could match any professional medium that he had ever seen.

Spiritualism had gotten its start in 1848 when two young girls claimed to communicate with the spirit of a dead peddler, which rapped out answers to questions in their father's rural New York farmhouse. The practice had gained wide acceptance by the late 1800s. Eminent men and women stated that they believed in the communication with the dead. Believers flocked to professional mediums, eager to contact lost loved ones. A talented medium could produce knocks and raps and conjure up words on ordinary slates. In many cases, spirit hands, faces and full-figured apparitions appeared before startled audiences.

Harry made his debut as a "spirit medium" on January 8, 1898 in the Galena, Kansas, opera house. Tied to a chair in his cabinet by a committee from the audience, he pretended to go into a trance. Once the curtains were closed, a mandolin played softly and bells and tambourines jangled before flying off over the heads of the crowd. When the curtains opened, Houdini was still firmly tied. Once more, the curtains closed and he was "freed from his bonds by the spirits."

When the applause died down, Houdini walked to the front of the stage and began to speak about the spirit world. He said that he could sense eerie presences on the stage. He closed and opened his eyes and gasped that messages were coming through from the other side. He named names, gave dates, told family secrets and sent chills down the spines of those who believed they had received communications from the dead.

Houdini had hurriedly prepared for this, the most convincing part of his performance, by listening to local gossip, reading back copies of the Galena newspaper, and copying names and dates from tombstones in local cemeteries. When Houdini pretended to contact the spirit of a black man whose throat had been cut and spelled out the victim's name, African-Americans in the gallery panicked and fled from the theater.

Dr. Hill was thrilled with the evening's performance and was in a fine mood as he totaled up the proceeds from the show. After that, a Sunday night séance was staged in every town on the circuit.

In Garnett, Kansas, Houdini delivered a spirit message to a woman who had recently lost her son. He told her not to grieve for the boy's spirit was calling to her, trying to tell her that he was happy. Soon, she would be blessed with another child to take his place. The woman, who was pregnant, was embarrassed and her husband was furious. He stormed backstage, grabbed Houdini and prepared to punch him in the face. Houdini talked fast, blurting out an incident from the man's past, which stunned the man so much that he let Harry go. The research that he had done into the family had saved him from a beating that, he later admitted, "I richly deserved."

An audience that came to see a séance, Houdini learned, was far easier to satisfy than one that came to see a magician. Those who believed in Spiritualism readily believed in messages from the dead. They were already convinced in the authenticity of the medium before they even arrived for the séance. Even skeptics were confounded by the accuracy of his revelations. The ruse of getting information beforehand was so simple that otherwise rational people refused to even consider a rational explanation for Houdini's "gifts."

The Sunday night séances greatly expanded Houdini's repertoire. He used his hands and feet adroitly in his escapes and now he practiced until he could pick up a piece of chalk between his toes and write on a slate that was placed beneath a table. He had seen armless entertainers in dime museums write, shave and play musical instruments with their feet but he had never tried to develop these skills himself.

Harry also mastered several table levitation techniques. One of the best, which was even then well known by several professional mediums, involved pressing firmly on the top of a table and forcing it to tip and balance on its left legs. Putting his right foot under the closest right table leg and clamping down with his right hand on the corner above it, he could make the table "float" by lifting his right foot. In the dark, with three spectators holding their fingertips lightly on the tabletop, the "levitation" had an uncanny effect. Afterward, the participants would swear that the table floated upward by psychic power alone -- and it rose even higher each time a sitter would re-tell the story.

While he was traveling with the show in St. Joseph, Missouri, Houdini was approached by several townspeople who asked him to expose a spiritualist who had been victimizing their friends. The medium, who had several excellent methods of getting information, agreed to meet with Houdini. The man was frank and honest with him. Of course he used tricks, he was a showman, just as Houdini was. The public wanted séances and he was giving them what they wanted. Contrary to what most people thought, he was making very little money with the scheme. He was almost broke. He planned to give one more séance to raise money and then he planned to pack up and leave town -- as long as Harry didn't expose him.

Houdini attended the séance with no plans to reveal the medium's secrets. He had the man's promise that he would leave town; that was enough. He decided to help make the last séance one to remember. Houdini later wrote, "While I had the table walking, someone threw a rock on it. I am satisfied that someone brought the rock along to help out the medium if he got in trouble. They [his supporters] were not taking any chances of his being unable to give a sign at the right time."

Houdini's spiritualism act became so popular that he was unable to get bookings as a magician. Harry and Bess soon began performing only as mediums. Sometimes Houdini varied his routine and used Bess as the voice of the spirits. They were in Canada when a spectator named Mary Murphy asked where her long-lost brother John could be found. Bess called out an address on East 72nd Street in New York. The next day, the woman returned with astonishing news that she had sent a telegram to New York and found her brother. Harry was amazed. How, he wanted to know, had Bess known the man would be there? Bess replied that she hadn't. The name Murphy reminded her of Mrs. Murphy's confectionary shop, a few blocks from their home on East 69th Street. This was the address that she had given. The fact that Mary Murphy's brother actually lived nearby was nothing more than a coincidence. Or was it? Paranormal enthusiasts have been debating this incident for many years. Some believe that it points to the idea that perhaps the Houdinis did have some latent psychic powers after all. Then again, it could have been a lucky guess. Who knows?

Another evening, in another town, Harry recognized a woman who had attended some of his séances scolding her son because he was reckless on his bicycle. The spirits sent her a message. Houdini described her son speeding down a hill. He lost control of his bike as he turned a corner. Houdini's face twisted. He now saw the boy, he said, walking with his arm hanging limply at his side. For a second time, a séance attendee returned with confirmation of the Houdini's psychic skills. The day after Harry spoke of the spirit message, the boy fell from his bicycle and broke his arm. Another coincidence? Or was it merely a good guess after seeing the boy being lectured about his reckless behavior?

Despite these eerie predictions, which caused a lot of talk, the Houdinis were still scarcely making enough money to live. This may have been because, despite the trickery of the séances, Houdini still had some scruples. He looked on his message reading and spirit manifestation act as just another phase of show business.

The medicine show tour ended and Houdini still found it difficult to book his magic and escape act. He and Bess eventually signed on to play another season with the Welsh Brothers Circus. At the end of the tour, the circus returned to its winter quarters in Pennsylvania and the Houdinis were given an enthusiastic letter of endorsement: "We can cheerfully recommend Harry and Beatrice Houdini with their unique and mysterious act called 'Metamorphosis' as being the strongest drawing card of its class in America. Their act is totally unlike others and always creates a profound impression... We will be pleased to play them at any time. The Houdinis are truly great people."

Despite this glowing praise, the Houdinis were no better off than they had been as cheap mediums. At twenty-four, Houdini was still on the bottom rung of the show business ladder. He promised his wife that he would try for one more year and then, if he was not a hit, he would give up magic and find another, more profitable, line of work.

"THE UNDISPUTED KING OF HANDCUFFS"

On January 5, 1899, a story about an unknown dime museum performer appeared on the front page of the *Chicago Journal*. A reporter had been at police headquarters when the magician, Harry Houdini, had boasted that he could release himself from any manacles. The cops quickly fastened him into restraints and, just as quickly, Houdini released himself. Police Sergeant Waldron locked Houdini into his own personal handcuffs at Kohl and Middleton's Clark Street Museum. This time, one of the cuffs withstood the escape artist's vigorous assault. When Waldron finally admitted that he had dropped a slug into the lock, Harry was furious.

While playing in St. Paul, Minnesota, early in 1899, Houdini was approached by a short, plump, German man after his show. Could Houdini, the man asked, free himself from other manacles, or only those used in the show? Houdini boasted that the restraint had yet to be made that could hold him. The next evening, the man returned with his own handcuffs, locked them on Houdini's wrists and pocketed the key. When the brash young magician easily escaped from the manacles, the man introduced himself as Martin Beck, the acclaimed booker for the Orpheum vaudeville circuit. He offered Houdini a trial date in Omaha if Harry would put together a new act with dramatic escapes.

Soon after, with Beck's assistance, Houdini left the small time behind and the enigmatic showman began his journey to become an American, and then a worldwide, sensation. In Omaha, where he played for a week and received $60 --- the most money he had ever earned at one time --- the escape artist began his trial run for the Orpheum circuit.

The magic tricks that had opened Houdini's dime museum and circus routines were dropped at Beck's insistence. He wanted Harry to make the emphasis of the act his ability to escape from nearly impregnable bonds.

When the curtain rose on his first show, the stage held six chairs and a table loaded with manacles. A trunk stood to one side at the back, and a large cabinet occupied center stage. The cabinet had a pipe framework with drapes on four sides and the top. Houdini began the show

Houdini finally began to make a name for himself with his Handcuff Challenge, daring audience members to produce a pair of cuffs from which he could not escape. Harry invented the challenge, which would soon have imitators across the country.

with a brief speech, stating that he would attempt to escape from the most difficult restraints ever created. He invited a committee of audience members to the stage, promising not to embarrass any of the volunteers. If anyone had brought their own handcuffs with which to challenge Houdini, they could bring those to the stage. The members of the committee were invited to examine the cabinet and to see for themselves that there was nothing concealed inside it. Harry picked up a pair of handcuffs from the table. They were regulation police irons, he assured the audience, used to hold dangerous criminals. A committee member examined the cuffs, and then locked them on Houdini's wrists. The spectator was told to put the key in his pocket and not to let it out of his possession. As Harry entered the cabinet, music began to play to build the excitement. In less than thirty seconds, Houdini emerged. The cuffs were still locked -- but they were no longer on his wrists. He tossed them to the committee. Next, several pairs of handcuffs and leg irons were shown and inspected, and Houdini identified each by name and gave a brief history of each of them. This escape took longer than the first and created more suspense.

The manacles were tested and made sure to be in working order. All of them were locked in place on Harry's arms and legs. Using a show of manly stress and strain, he tugged at them and looked worried as he entered the cabinet. Music, which started slowly and then increased in speed until it was nearly a frenzy, stopped abruptly as the drapes of the enclosure were pulled aside and Houdini walked out, free of the chains.

The act continued to an applause-producing finish, ending with the "Metamorphosis" escape, during which Harry slipped out of a wrist tie, a knotted bag and a roped and locked trunk in three seconds. When the trunk's lid was raised, Bess was found tied in his place.

Challenges at every performance added drama to the proceedings. He hired men who were given handcuffs from his collection and told to sit in the audience. If no legitimate challengers appeared, these men immediately came forward.

Houdini proudly proclaimed himself to be the originator of the handcuff challenge act. The challenge element of the act lifted it from the dime museum and small-time level to the big-time vaudeville show. The challenger performer, by necessity, had to be familiar with every type of iron, and to know how to open handcuffs without his methods being detected. Houdini spent endless off-stage hours working with locksmiths, learning the secrets of the trade. He read every book he could find on the subject. He visited museums and police stations and studied both old and new restraints. Duplicate keys could open any manacle and even better were picks made of twisted wire and bent steel. They were smaller than keys and easier to conceal. Houdini's skills as a magician and his ability to palm, misdirect attention, and hide his picks in unlikely places were invaluable assets.

While Houdini was becoming well-known for his handcuff escapes, the "Metamorphosis" illusion remained a highlight of the act, if for no other reason than the speed in which Harry and Bess could pull it off!

In Omaha, Houdini managed to slip out of five pairs of regulation handcuffs and a set of official leg irons that were dramatically supplied by the police department. Impressed by the enthusiastic report from the theater manager, Martin Beck signed Houdini for the Orpheum circuit tour. By the time he reached California, his salary had jumped to $90.

In San Francisco, Houdini was stripped to the skin in the office of the San Francisco detective force and examined by a police surgeon. He then proceeded to slip out of ten pairs of handcuffs, a wide leather belt used to subdue dangerous prisoners and a regulation straitjacket. The escapes took place behind the closed door of a closet and the veteran detectives could come up

Houdini began earning a reputation for escaping from jail cells in the cities he visited on tour. When he arrived, he began to be challenged by the local police to escape from one of their cells. If they didn't, he challenged them and never failed. These escapes soon became a standard publicity stunt for every town he visited.

with no explanation as to how it was done. The lengthy newspaper account failed to mention that Houdini had visited the detective bureau in advance to inspect the restraints and likewise never mentioned the kiss he exchanged with Bess prior to being placed in the closet. There was no way that they could know about that Bess slipped a key to her husband with her tongue in the midst of their kiss!

When Houdini's salary soared to $150 per week, he ran large ads in the trade papers to make sure that the theatrical world knew of his accomplishments. Martin Beck used the ads, as well as the lengthy newspapers stories chronicling his feats and box office reports from the Orpheum tour, to sell Houdini to the Keith Theater circuit as a headliner.

To publicize his first date at the Orpheum Theatre in Kansas City, Houdini escaped from handcuffs at the Central Police Station. When he returned after playing the Keith theaters, he introduced his second major publicity stunt. Stripped naked, fastened at his wrists and ankles by five pairs of irons, he was locked in a cell and in less than eight minutes, he escaped from not only the manacles but the cell, too. Needless to say, newspaper headlines screamed his name and Houdini rode the wave of popularity to several sold-out shows.

By the end of the Keith run, Houdini had money in the bank and his scrapbooks were filled with newspaper stories, official letters from police departments verifying his escapes, and theater advertisements and playbills with top billing.

Harry's mother, Cecilia, couldn't have been happier. She was sure that after his great success, her son would be able to spend more time at home with her. But this was not to be the case. Harry was about to make the biggest gamble of his life and it would be months, perhaps years, before he would see his mother again.

AN AMERICAN MAGICIAN ABROAD

Convinced that he could make it in Europe and eager to travel abroad, Harry and Bess sailed to England on May 30, 1900. They arrived in London without a single booking, taking an enormous chance that Houdini would amaze European audiences in the same way that he did American ones. He met with dubious theater managers, who leafed through his scrapbooks, read his reviews and his testimonials from police officials and watched him slip out of handcuffs. All of them were non-committal, telling him that when he performed, they would come and see him. One door after another was closed to him, until he met a young theatrical agent who was just starting out in the business named Harry Day. Without a long list of other performers on his roster, Day eagerly met with the magician. Charmed by his confidence and accomplishments, he arranged for Houdini to audition at the famed Alhambra Theater.

C. Dundas Slater, the theater manager, was impressed by Houdini's skill but was dubious that he could escape from any restraints other than the ones used in the act. Slater suggested that Harry pay a visit to Scotland Yard. Harry, eager for such an opportunity, quickly agreed. At the Yard, Superintendent Melville instructed Houdini to put his arms around a sturdy pillar. He locked a pair of manacles on Harry's wrists to hold him in place, then he ushered Slater to the door. They would return, Melville said, when the young man had exhausted himself. Before the door had closed behind them, a shout and a clatter prompted Melville to turn around. The Scotland Yard cuffs were on the floor. Houdini was leaning against the post, free of the cuffs.

Houdini quickly received his first British contract.

In July 1900, he opened to acclaim at the Alhambra Theater in London and then traveled to Germany, where he set new box-office records in Dresden and Berlin. The demand for vaudeville handcuff acts became so great that he brought his brother Theo from New York and sent him on tour as "Hardeen." Within a year, Houdini was the most popular attraction in Europe.

Harry and Bess in Germany

Houdini never turned down any opportunity for publicity. When Werner Graf, a German policeman, wrote a derisive article in July 1901, accusing Houdini of lying when he said that he could escape from any sort of police restraint, Houdini sued Graf for slander. He fought the case through two German appeals courts but he eventually won the case. Houdini celebrated by issuing a new advertising lithograph picturing him in a tuxedo and manacles, standing before the highest German tribunal. The lithograph was titled "Apologize in the name of King Wilhelm II, Kaiser of Germany," and it included a few words on Graf's forced apology and the fact that he had to pay all of the magician's court costs.

Houdini loved publicity and he was never the sort to ignore an insult. Engelberto Klepini, an escape artist with the Circus Sidoli, advertised in 1902 that he had defeated the American in a handcuff competition. He likely assumed that Houdini would never see the advertisement but not only did Harry see it, he traveled from Holland to Dortmund, Germany, to confront his detractor in person. Wearing a disguise, he took a seat in the stands. He sat through the show until Klepini told the audience he had beaten Houdini in an escape contest. At that point, Harry leapt into the circus ring, ripped off his disguise and, waving a handful of bank notes, challenged the startled performer. He would give Klepini 5,000 marks if he could escape from a pair of Houdini handcuffs --- and he would offer another 5,000 if Houdini could not escape from his!

Prodded by the circus' business manager, Klepini agreed to allow Houdini to lock him into a set of French letter cuffs the next night. Before show time, the business manager was shown the manacles and Houdini showed him how they could be opened by turning the five cylinders to spell out c-l-e-f-s, the French word for keys. Klepini confidently entered his cabinet but after thirty minutes, the structure was moved to the side of the ring so that the rest of the show could continue. After the program ended, workers lifted the cabinet again. Klepini ran out and darted across the ring to the manager's office --- still shackled. It was almost 1:00 a.m. when the manager ordered Klepini to give up. Harry spun the cylinders until the letters f-r-a-u-d fell into place. The cuffs sprang open. He had changed the combination before the manacles were placed on his competitor's wrists.

If the police did not challenge Houdini in a city where he played, Houdini challenged them. During an engagement in Moscow in May 1903, he dared the chief of the Russian secret police, Inspector Lebedoeff, to imprison him on one of the "escape-proof" jails on wheels that had been designed to transport enemies of the state to Siberia. Houdini had seen one of these strange horse-drawn vans on the street and had examined it while the horses were drinking from a trough. Escape was impossible from the front, sides, bottom or top but the entrance door at the back was fastened with a single padlock located just below a barred window that a slender arm could pass through.

There were no reporters present on May 11 when he was stripped and searched. Harry said that it was the most trying examination that he ever endured. Two iron bands, joined by a short metal bar, were padlocked on his wrists. A pair of fetters, linked by a chain, were enclosed around his ankles. He was locked inside the wagon, and then it was turned in the prison courtyard so that the door faced away from Lebedoeff and his staff.

It took Harry twenty-eight minutes to get free. The police were furious. They ran around the wagon to the door and found it still locked. Inside, on the metal floor, were the shackles that had been locked on Houdini's arms and legs. Houdini was seized and searched again, even more thoroughly than before. Then they turned on Franz Kukol, the owner of the theater where Houdini was appearing. He had been kept at some distance from the wagon but he was stripped and searched anyway. Nothing was found.

Houdini asked Lebedoeff to sign a document that verified his escape but the chief of the secret police refused. It was bad enough that Houdini had set himself free; Lebedoeff was not about to publicize that fact. Despite this, news spread throughout the city. Houdini's month-long booking was extended to eight weeks. Handsome lithographs began to appear showing the American magician outwitting the Russian secret police.

One of the high points of Houdini's life had nothing to do with performing death-defying feats. While in England, he purchased an elegant dress said to have been made for Queen Victoria. He arranged a grand reception where he presented his mother in the dress to all their relatives. He said it was the happiest day of his life.

It was around this time, in 1904, that he paid $125,000 for a newly built, four-story brownstone at 278 W. 113th St. in Harlem for $25,000. When he and Bess moved in with Cecilia it was in a predominantly German and Jewish neighborhood.

Having returned to America, Houdini and found himself in great demand. His exploits in Europe had been widely reported at home and he was soon selling out theaters all over the country. He also found that a number of imitators had appeared during the years that he was abroad.

Robert Cunningham, who had shortened his name to Cunning, was the most successful of the escapologists who sprang up in American vaudeville during the five years that Houdini performed in Europe. Cunning erroneously claimed to have traveled the globe, gathering his magical skills, and was now the greatest handcuff and jail escape artist in the world.

Houdini and his brother Dash, still calling himself Hardeen, were in the audience on September 11, 1905 when Cunning appeared at Hyde and Behmen's Theater in Brooklyn.

Houdini: Among the Spirits - Page 28

Hardeen was one of five men who brought manacles to the stage at Cunning's request. The fetters offered by the others were accepted but Cunning took one look at Theo's manacles and refused to put them on. Not only had he stolen his act from Houdini, but he even stole the other magician's line when he decided not to use the cuffs, "These cuffs are not regulation." Theo pulled a banknote from his pocket and said that it would go to charity if Cunning escaped from his cuffs. The theater manager came out of the wings and bet $100 of his own money that Cunning would succeed. Cunning shook his head and pushed the cuffs back into Theo's hands, bringing on a wave of hoots and jeers from the audience. The fire curtain suddenly came down and someone threw a punch at Hardeen. He struck back and for a moment, it seemed an all-out brawl was going to break out. A policeman pushed his way through the melee, arrested Dash and took him to the station house. He was charged with disorderly conduct. Houdini put up his bail money. The next day, a judge heard the case and dismissed it, commenting that it was obviously a publicity stunt.

Cunning sensed more trouble at Hurtig and Seamon's Music Hall on 125th Street in Harlem. He told the audience that one of his challengers was a rival's brother. The man insisted that his handcuffs be accepted and the audience shouted for Cunning to comply. Against his better judgment, the beleaguered Cunning agreed. He allowed seven pairs of manacles to be locked on his wrists and arms and then stepped into a cage-like cabinet. A cloth was draped over it. There was a long wait and the spectators grew more restless by the minute. They were yelling insults when Cunning finally emerged from the cabinet with only one of his wrists freed. The challenger shouted that he wanted his handcuffs back and again, there was bedlam. The fire curtain slammed down to the stage and the challenger tried to get behind it. Stagehands shoved him back. He still managed to push backstage but four men grabbed him and hustled him out to the lobby. He waited until his irons were returned and then he shouted, "They're ruined! The teeth have been filed off!" The manager of the theater had him arrested. When the case came up, the man was identified as William Weiss. The charge was dismissed and Houdini's older brother went free.

Houdini's younger brother, Dr. Leopold Weiss, journeyed all over New England plaguing imitation performers with Harry's "defeater" cuffs. Houdini, who regarded himself as the originator of the challenge escape act, insisted that anyone who imitated it was a thief.

To stir up excitement in America, Harry devised a novel press stunt. The New York papers said that Houdini would compete with his pupil, "Jacques Boudini," in an underwater escape contest. Each was wagering $500 on the outcome and the winner would take all. A tugboat took them out into the New York harbor on September 20. Both men were shackled hand and foot, tied with ropes, and dropped overboard.

For a minute and thirty seconds, newsmen and photographers saw only ripples on the water's surface. Then Houdini's head popped up and he spat out a stream of water. He asked if "Boudini" was up yet and was told that he wasn't. Harry surged up out of the water, waved his hands to show they were free, and then sank out of view. A minute later, he bobbed up again. He gasped for breath, looked around and then went under again. Another minute and then he reappeared and asked about his competitor, who had still not appeared. Harry laughed and kicked a leg in the air to show that one of his ankles was free. He went under once more and came back up a minute later to show that he was completely free of his bonds. He swam to the side of the boat and was lifted out of the water.

"Boudini," who appeared to be more dead than alive, was retrieved from the water. His manacles were still in place. After artificial respiration, he opened his eyes and mumbled, " I swallowed some water." The tugboat steamed back to the dock. Only two of the reporters were not duped into believing the stunt had been real. They knew it was simply a showcase for Houdini's skill -- but it didn't matter. It was the sort of story that people liked to read.

When Houdini opened at the Colonial Theater in Manhattan his years of performing in Europe had sharpened his skills, his showmanship and his timing. His dynamic stage presence quickly won over audiences and after two weeks at the Colonial and another two weeks at the Orpheum, he went on tour. Business was tremendous in Detroit, Cleveland, Rochester and Buffalo, but it was not until he reached Washington, D.C., that he struck publicity gold.

In Washington, he staged his most remarkable prison break so far. In March 1906, officials locked the naked magician in a cell on "Murderer's Row" that had once held Charles Guiteau, the assassin of President James Garfield. The officers then locked Harry's clothes in another cell and returned to the warden's office. Working quickly, Houdini freed himself and then proceeded to open all of the doors and to shift the prisoners from one cell to another. He met no resistance, and in fact, the prisoners were highly entertained, although surprised by the sudden appearance of a naked man. After changing the cells of all of the men on the entire cellblock, Harry locked the cells, got dressed and knocked on the warden's door. The entire feat took less than twenty-seven minutes.

Two signed documents verified the amazing incident -- one by the warden and the other by Major Richard Sylvester, the prison superintendent. Sylvester's document said in part: "The experiment was a valuable one in that the department has been instructed as to the adoption of further security which will protect any lock from being opened or interfered with." Houdini's suggestions -- and the feat itself -- effectively blocked any future rival who wanted to duplicate the stunt.

Houdini's most publicized Boston escape was made on March 19 from the Tombs in New York City. He broke out of Cell 60, entered Cell 77, where he dressed. Then, instead of going to the superintendent's office he ran across the prison yard, climbed the Somerset Street wall, vaulted an iron railing, and hurried through the snow to his dressing room at the theater. He telephoned the Tombs to give them the news of his escape. Startled newspaper reporters insisted that he return to the jail so that photographs of his exploit could be taken for the papers.

Between shows once night, he went to Cambridge, Massachusetts, and performed at the Harvard Union. He slipped out of a pair of handcuffs, a straitjacket and a roped chair. He cut the rope into small pieces and gave them out to the students as souvenirs.

On March 25, he performed at the Boston Athletic Club. He also lectured on his travels and displayed many of the relics that he had collected over the years. He spoke of the Hindu fakirs that he had studied over the years, dismissing those who believed they worked miracles. Anyone could duplicate their feats -- with practice. He pushed a long steel needle into his cheek without drawing blood to illustrate what he meant. There was no deception involved. Houdini had learned the feat during his dime museum days. He ended his performance with his straitjacket escape, which brought the audience to its feet.

After the show, Houdini was given a head-to-toe examination by Dr. J.E. Rourke, anatomist at Massachusetts General Hospital. The doctor, who had examined a number of human oddities and circus strongmen, was eager to see how Houdini's arduous work had affected his body. He pronounced Harry to be in excellent physical shape, capable of incredible activity and able to harden his muscles to sustain strenuous blows. The doctor predicted that the magician would live to be a very old man.

Despite his full schedule in Boston, Houdini found time to publish a small book called "The Right Way to Do Wrong," which revealed the methods of burglars, pickpockets, bunco men and spirit mediums. The book sold well at Houdini's shows but it earned criticism from some corners. A man named A.F. Hill wrote to Houdini about this book. "You are advertised as if you intended to expose some evil in astrology, clairvoyance, mediumship, etc. Fake mediums are not any worse than a mechanical fake magician. I have seen you perform, but what good are you to society?"

He also suffered another painful barb when the *New York Sun* ran a short account of his escape from the Yorkville police court jail. The officers there, the story said, watched Houdini through a peephole and saw him take something from between the toes of his right foot and use it, as he reached his arm through the bars, to open the Yale lock on the cell door.

Dr. Albert M. Wilson, the editor of the magicians' journal, *Sphinx*, had little use for Houdini and printed the story, adding that Houdini was "swelling out his chest like a pouter pigeon, protruding his abdomen like a cormorant and dropping calumny from his lips like the malodorous emanations from the glands of a Mustelidae mephitis."

The public not only did not share Wilson's opinion, they very likely had no idea that in the last case, he was referring to a skunk. In 1906 Houdini started his own magazine but the Conjurer's Monthly went out of business after only two years. His performances, however, continued to draw enormous crowds. Five times as many people saw Houdini in Pittsburgh in October 1906 at the Grand Theater as attended Ethel Barrymore's performances at the Nixon Theater across town. His offstage publicity kept his name in the news. In the course of a naked jailbreak at the Allegheny Central Police Station, Houdini switched a deserter from the 11th U.S. Infantry from one cell to another. The soldier reportedly gaped at the nude intruder and asked where he had left his clothes. Harry replied, "I pawned them."

ATTEMPTING THE IMPOSSIBLE

A tempestuous period began for Houdini on November 26, 1906. While playing at Detroit's Temple Theater, he refused to accept a challenge to escape from handcuffs presented by a policeman named Alphonse Baker. They were not in proper working order, Harry said, and had been rigged to defeat him. The audience shouted at him to try them anyway and Houdini agreed. As he walked, manacled, to the cabinet, he spotted a bookkeeper and part-time magician named Harrison L. Davies in an upper box. He called out to Davies and asked him if the cuffs were his work, but Davies shook his head no.

Houdini struggled in the box for an hour and thirty-five minutes. Long before he was free, Bess left the stage in tears. The *Detroit Journal* reported that her tears turned to hysterics in the dressing room. As Houdini returned the handcuffs to the police officer, he asked if they were his personal manacles. No, Baker replied, another Detroit man had asked him to take them to the stage.

A short time later, Deputy Sheriff James V. Cunningham offered $100 to anyone who could successfully break out of the Wayne County jail. Houdini inspected the cellblock before he took the wager. When he saw that a single sliding bar locked every cellblock in the row, he knew that escape was impossible without assistance. He could pick a lock that could be reached through the bar, but when the control lever was at the end of the corridor, he was helpless.

To recover from his embarrassment, he announced that he would make a dangerous bridge leap. On the morning of the feat, Houdini and Franz Kukol, his assistant, went to the police storage barn and borrowed a coil of heavy rope. While there, he hastily scrawled his will on the back of an envelope: "I give it all to Bess." Several officers added their names below his signature as witnesses. He passed the envelope to Kukol for safekeeping.

The two men traveled out to the Belle Island Bridge and despite the winter weather, many

Detroiters came on their lunch hour to see the spectacle. Harry stood at the railing and stripped off all of his clothes except for his trousers. He shivered in the raw air as two pairs of police handcuffs were fastened to his wrists and one end of a safety rope was tied around his waist. He posed briefly for photographers before he jumped into the cold water twenty-five feet below.

A loud gasp went up from the crowd on the bridge and the shoreline as he body sailed through the air and vanished beneath the surface of the river. There were cheers as he surfaced, waved the released cuffs in his hands and swam over to a waiting boat.

Bess hadn't known about the bridge jump until her smiling and wet husband returned to their room at the St. Clair Hotel. She was furious with him. A bridge leap in warm weather was bad enough but on a bitterly cold day, it was ridiculous. Harry obviously had no regard for himself, but he needed to consider his wife once in a while. After her tirade was over, she helped him to undress and change into some dry, warm clothes. That afternoon, at the Temple Theater, he performed for a packed house that had been attracted by the front page news stories of the underwater escape. They cheered as the magician escaped from a packing case in just nine minutes.

Although legend had it that the underwater escape occurred in Detroit on December 2, and that a hole had to be cut in the ice on the river's surface for Harry to jump through, the feat actually took place on November 27 and the temperature was well above freezing. It was certainly cold, although the stories of how he had swam in circles underwater until he was able to find a place in the ice that he could break through and make it to the surface was undoubtedly enhanced to make the feat seem more exciting.

In December, Louis Paul, a Midwestern escape artist, challenged Houdini with a pair of handcuffs at the Majestic Theater in Chicago. Harry convinced the audience that the manacles were fixed and he, in turn, challenged Paul to escape from an "unhampered-with" pair. Paul refused and was booed off the stage. A man who identified himself as a special detective from the Central Police Station offered irons that Houdini examined and approved. Harry turned so that the man could lock them behind his back -- then worked for nearly an hour and a half before he was able to free himself. The theater, which usually closed hours earlier, stayed open that night until midnight. Once free, Houdini examined the cuffs again. The closer he looked, the angrier he got. He showed the audience how an extra rivet had been added to try and prevent his escape. He shouted at the man that he had switched the cuffs. The irons that had been locked on his wrists were not the same ones that he had inspected before the stunt. Several audience members seized the man and searched him. They found a second, matching pair, in his pocket.

A review about the show appeared in the *Chicago Daily News*, "For years there has not been such a sensation as Houdini. His coming into the ranks for vaudeville brings a new light which is not likely to be extinguished by the army of imitators, of apes, of envious fakers." The critic, Amy Leslie, described Houdini's straitjacket release, "He battled with the canvas prison, tore at its leather and writhed, squirmed, crept and twisted like a tortured thing of muscles and emotion and no bones. Suddenly George Ade turned to me when I imagined I was most calm and said 'Gee, you're having a worse time than Houdini.'"

On January 4, 1907, Houdini took on the University of Pennsylvania football team, so to speak. While he was onstage at the Chestnut Street Theater in Philadelphia, the entire squad, in their uniforms, jogged down the aisle with a giant football and lifted it over the footlights. Then they manacled Houdini, bent him double to fit into an opening on the ball, and stuffed him inside. The ball was laced with chains and padlocked. Harry escaped in just thirty-five minutes.

Houdini returned to Keith's Theater in Boston for the last three weeks of the month. He was bound to a ladder by five men who spent fifteen minutes chaining him and locking him into place. He escaped in seven minutes. When he was booked back into the theater in February, six riveters sealed him into a galvanized iron boiler. The process used to seal the boiler, with blowtorches and spurting flames, was a

At Keith's Theater in Boston, a committee of five men spent fifteen minutes chaining and locking Harry to a ladder. He escaped in half the time it took to lock him up!

show in itself. A full hour passed before Harry emerged, his hands and face covered with soot, his shirt collar gone, and his hair wildly disheveled. Another night, employees of the Derby Desk Company pushed a six-foot-long roll top desk onto the stage. The removed the upper storage compartments and blotter rack and put Houdini inside. The desk was locked at eight minutes past ten. At shortly before eleven, Harry added another escape to his list of victories.

Houdini toured all over the country in 1907 but on the opening day of a two-week engagement at the Columbia Theater in St. Louis in January 1908, the manager bluntly informed him that his act wouldn't mean a thing for the box office. Receipts for the first week were below par and so Harry opened the second week, January 27, 1908, with a new blockbuster mystery that he had been holding in reserve for just such an occasion. It was the first of the escapes for which he would become world famous -- from a padlocked water can.

A committee inspected the large, airtight, galvanized iron container. It was similar in shape to the milk cans that dairies supplied to farmers but was large enough -- just barely -- to hold a man. While the can was being filled with water, Harry went offstage to put on his bathing suit. The volunteers looked on as assistants filled the container with water. While this was being done, Houdini was building the drama by grimly reminding the audience that a man could only live for a short time without "life-sustaining air." He suggested that they start holding their breath the moment that his head disappeared from view into the tank. He entered the can feet first and quickly disappeared. Water spilled out over the sides of the container and extra bucketfuls were added to fill the can to the top.

As Harry descended from view, most of the onlookers held their breath. Within thirty seconds, most of them were gasping for air but Houdini had not appeared. He stayed out for sight for nearly two minutes. This act of endurance won him a large round of applause, but the most thrilling part of the act was still to come. This time, before Houdini went back into the water-filled can, his wrists were handcuffed. More water was added until the can overflowed onto the stage. Quickly, his assistants jammed the top onto the can and secured it with six padlocks. Escape seemed impossible.

A curtain was drawn around the can and time began to tick by. Audience members who had again gulped in a large breath of air as Houdini vanished into the can now gasped for air with loud, whopping coughs. The clocked ticked --- thirty seconds passed, then sixty, then ninety. Franz Kukol came from backstage with an ax in his hands, prepared to break the locks to save the magician. He

Houdini began what became his famous water can escapes at a theater in St. Louis in 1908. They would be his most popular for several years, until the invention of his Chinese Underwater Torture Escape was unveiled.

leaned toward the curtain and listened closely, but there was no sound. Two minutes passed, then three. Kukol raised the ax. The tension in the theater was nearly unbearable. Something must have gone terribly wrong. Audience members began shouting to the assistants on the stage, urging them to break open the locks and to free Houdini! Finally, Kukol leaned forward with the ax and started to pull back the curtain around the milk can. Just as he did, though, Houdini, dripping wet but wearing a wide smile, ripped the curtain aside and stepped out into full view. As he took a bow, the rafters of the theater quaked from the sound of the audience applause.

Thrilled with the success of his new feature, Harry had a shock waiting for him in Cleveland. When he saw the billboards outside the theater, he was shocked. At the top was "Mr. Julius Steger," the actor who would appear in a dramatic sketch, "The Fifth Commandment." His eyes went to the bottom of the bill, where he found his name. It was printed larger than Steger's, but his week was ruined anyway.

His ego took another blow later in New York when he read the review of his act in the *New York American*. Alan Dale, a critic who had seen him performing at the Alhambra in London while on vacation abroad and who had written a scathing review of him there, was after him again. Harry pasted the horrible review in a scrapbook along with his glowing notices, to read whenever he felt he was getting too full of himself:

The "famous" Houdini is a clever manipulator of handcuffs who appears to suffer in the very worst way from that terrible and baffling disease -- the swollen head. Houdini devoted the greater part of his "turn" to talking about himself in a cheap and rather pitiful way. It was as dull as ditch water. A good deal of his poor talk was "gallery play" -- what a hard time he had of it in England, how they hated to see him earning money over there, how cruelly jealous they were of him in Blackburn, but that he'd go back there and get more money. If he doesn't do a better turn in Blackburn than he did in Harlem, I don't fancy that he'll succeed in his design of "getting more money". This was all piffle and sad piffle.

Years ago I saw this really clever young man in London and was delighted with what I saw, but now it all seems spoiled. Even the particularly effective parlor trick in which Houdini is apparently padlocked into a huge can of water, from which he successfully "emerges" in his cabinet, is marred by the offensive manners of the man.

Far from being "delighted" in London, Dale had actually written that he "preferred Houdini's literature to his turn." He also said that the handcuff escapes were "spoiled" because they were made under the cover of a cabinet. Regardless of the review, the crowds ignored it and Houdini managed to fill the theater every night during his run.

INTO THE AIR

After performing in Boston, where he played sold-out shows and made an amazing escape after leaping from a bridge over the Charles River, Harry and Bess sailed for Germany in August 1908. When Cecelia Weiss returned from seeing them off from the docks, she wound the grandfather clock in the living room of her home on West 113th Street. It remained mute while her son was at home. Now, when she heard it chime and strike the hour, she knew that each minute that passed would hasten his return to her.

Houdini opened in Berlin in September and the challenge handcuff routine was missing from his act. He would never feature it again. The army of imitators around the world had destroyed its commercial value and left a bad taste in Harry's mouth. Now, his features were an out-in-the-open straitjacket escape and the water-filled, padlocked milk can. Between the two, he offered a number of illusions, including the "East Indian Needle Trick," in which he appeared to swallow fifty to one hundred needles and twenty yards of thread and bring them up threaded. The stunt brought show-stopping applause.

While at the Oxford Theatre in London, Harry received one of his most unusual challenges from five Chinese sailors. They mailed a letter to him and when he didn't reply, they published the challenge in the *Star*. The newspaper reported that it was written in Chinese and was nearly a yard long. When translated, it dared the escape artist to release himself from the "Sanguaw," a torture device used to punish criminals in China. In its most vicious form, the victim's feet were nailed to vertical shafts of wood while leather straps held their bodies motionless and a chain from an upper crossbar garroted their necks.

After the challenge was printed in English, Harry said that he would accept the challenge as long as his feet didn't actually have to be nailed to the wood. He also requested two doctors be allowed on stage to ensure that he didn't strangle while in the device. He said that he would have to inspect the mechanism and if he didn't succeed in escaping in full view, he would be given the opportunity to try again in a private room.

Harry went with a reporter from the *Star* to Limehouse to view the torture instrument.

Before returning to England, Harry performed in Boston and made a jump from the Harvard Bridge into the Charles River.

Apparently, it met with his approval, for on the next night, Friday, November 20, the five Asian men, in Western clothing but wearing long, braided hair, set up the torture device on the stage at the Oxford. Attached to the solid base were two slanting posts that supported a crossbar considerably wider than the base. The structure resembled an inverted triangle. The sailors crossed Houdini's feet and strapped his ankles with a thick leather strap. Four chains extended outward from this strap and were pulled taut and nailed at the ends to the floor. Houdini's neck was encircled by a tangle of rusty chains. The chains were tightened and the ends were nailed to the extremities of the upper crossbar. Finally, his wrists were strapped together and the far ends of the chains attached to the strap were nailed to the tapering sides of the structure.

Houdini went to work but five minutes of strenuous struggles only managed to yank a nail, which held a chain to the upright, out of place. The nail was pounded back into the wood and the struggle began again. Bit by bit, he managed to ease his left foot out of his shoe. The shoe fell to the stage. Then, his right foot clattered to the boards. He uncrossed his ankles in the strap that bound them and pulled his left foot up and out. Soon, his right foot was also free. The strap and chains banged down on the floor. With an agile leap, he swung his body up until he caught the top bar between his legs. He pulled himself up until he was astride the bar. Carefully perched there, he used his teeth on the buckles of the straps that bound his hands. When he managed to slip his hands out, he used them to loosen his neck from the chains and he jumped down to the stage -- just sixteen minutes after he had been tethered into place. He made the escape seem easy but Houdini was quick to confess to the Star reporter that he would never accept the "Sanguaw" torture test again.

A short time later, Harry accepted another challenge for an escape to be made in full view. He was strapped, laced, and roped into a "Crazy Crib" by three men who worked as attendants in London insane asylums. Harry had seen his first "Crazy Crib" in 1896 in the same Canadian institution where the struggles of an inmate in a straitjacket had inspired him to attempt the escape on stage. At the time, he had also devised a method of escape when shackled to a bed with handcuffs and leg irons. In those days, he thought a canopy was necessary to hide his struggles from the audience. Now, his contortions caused the audience as much excitement as his out-in-the-open straitjacket feat.

Two weeks later, six suffragettes (women dedicated to winning the right to vote) wrapped

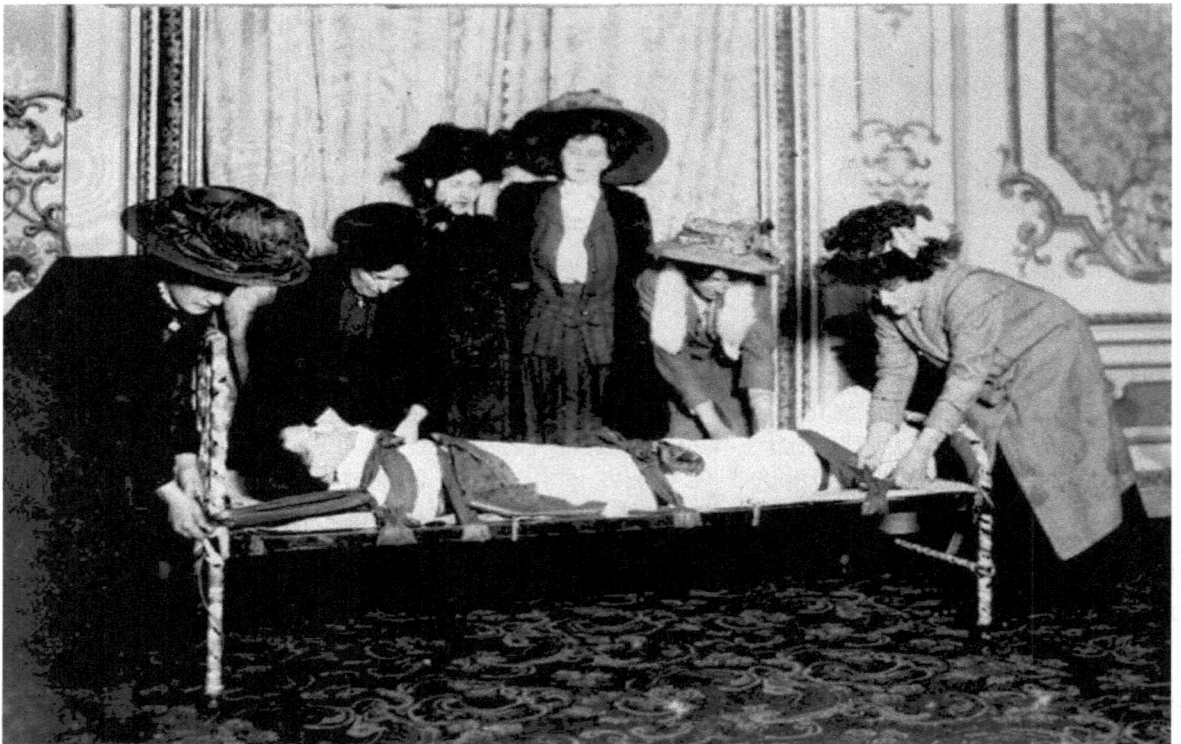

Six suffragettes bound Houdini to a "crazy crib" bed on the London stage. When one of them kissed him while he was in his restraints, it was probably the only time Harry ever blushed on stage.

Houdini in sheets and bound him to a mattress with bandages. Once the women were sure that he was securely tied, one of them bent down and kissed him. It was probably the only time that Harry ever blushed on stage.

Houdini's run in London broke box office records at both the Oxford Theatre and the Euston, located in another part of the city. He accepted a challenge from William Jordan & Sons on December 2 and escaped from one of their milk churns rather than his usual water can.

Two nights later, he took on a test with a safe. Accounts of this escape have gained legendary proportions. It has been written that the safe was so heavy that braces had to be erected under the stage to support it and that it was large enough to hold three standing men. The release, according to one story, took Houdini forty-five minutes. In truth, the safe was a small one -- a genuine old burglar-proof safe, which could easily hold a single human being. According to Houdini, it took only fourteen minutes for him to escape.

Houdini jumped from the upper deck of a tugboat into the Mersey River in Liverpool on December 7. He was weighted down by twenty-two pounds of chains and irons. He was up in forty-five seconds. The next week in Birmingham, he jumped from a houseboat, moored in the Edgbaston Reservoir during a driving rainstorm. He slipped out of his manacles in forty-two seconds.

In Scotland, the Dundee police refused to give Harry permission to jump from the parapet of the Tay Bridge. Hundreds of spectators had showed up to watch and rather than disappoint them, Harry boarded a pleasure boat and, after being chained and manacled, jumped from the ship's bridge. He was free from his chains and above the water in thirty seconds.

During his engagement at the Alhambra Theater in Paris in April 1909, still frustrated because the French police refused to allow him to escape from their jails, Houdini sent letters to the press and to theater managers inviting them to meet him at the Pont de l'Archeveche, the "Archbishop's Bridge" that crossed the Seine River. Harry arrived by automobile just before 3:00 p.m. and brought with him a French private detective and several reporters. Houdini pulled off his coat, trousers, tie, shirt, shoes and socks. Clad only in a swimsuit, he extended his hands and the detective shackled them and locked a chain around his neck. His assistants erected a folding ladder and in seconds, Harry was atop the wall of the Paris Morgue. He jumped up and down, yelled and waved his manacled arms. Soon, thousands of puzzled Frenchmen were pointing out the madman to their neighbors. Still and movie cameramen along with Houdini's assistants set up their cameras and focused on the spectacle. Excited watchers were calling for the police when Houdini jumped off the wall and plunged into the waters of the Seine. Once the cameramen had recorded the escape, Harry swam to the shore, slipped into an overcoat and escaped in a waiting car.

Returning to England in early June, Houdini was seen by Harry Rickards, Australia's leading vaudeville booker. He was in London on a booking expedition and saw Houdini's show at the Chelsea Music Hall when three challenges were met. Overflow seats were sold on the stage and hundreds were turned away at the door. The show, and the audience's response to it, convinced Rickards to offer Harry a contract in Australia. It would pay him the largest sum ever paid to a performer for a season down under. His opening was set for February of the following year.

Houdini was booked too far ahead to accept an earlier contract.

Harry's principal irritant in England during this trip was a man named John Clempert, a showman who had once been a professional wrestler and then "The Man They Cannot Hang." Dangling by his legs from a trapeze, Clempert would attach a rope to his neck, then release his hold on the trapeze with his legs. After a breathtaking fifteen-foot fall, he would hang by his neck in the air. One night, however, his fall was just a little too sharp and he seriously injured his spine. While in bed recuperating, he later said, he knew he would never be able to wrestle or do his rope trick again, so he hit upon the idea of a handcuff, chain, rope and trunk act. Clempert's "original" act had him escape from riveted boilers and packing cases and jumping off bridges. Newspapers noted that in addition to duplicating Houdini's act as closely as he could, he was also exploiting the Milk Can feat. One writer noted, "Clempert is 'the man they could not hang.' Perhaps this is a pity..."

Since theater entertainments could be copyrighted in Great Britain, Houdini filed suit against Clempert. When his rival swore that he would discontinue stealing Houdini's feats, Harry dropped the court case and Clempert faded away from the public eye.

Houdini continued performing in England and, too busy to return to New York for a summer holiday, he brought his mother and Bess' mother to England for a visit. Mrs. Rahner had finally warmed up to her son-in-law during his last American tour. Better still, she and Mrs. Weiss, once they met, thoroughly enjoyed each other's company.

Later that summer, Harry traveled to Germany to perform. While at the Hansa Theater in Hamburg, a news item appeared that announced an aviator named Grade was going to show off his skills in a French biplane. Houdini was very interested. Aviation was one of his current obsessions and he had once offered $5,000 for the use of the Wright brothers' airplane. He planned to be handcuffed and flown over London's West End. He would then parachute down, escaping from his manacles on the way, and land in Piccadilly Circus. The flight was canceled due to technical difficulties.

Houdini hired a car to take him to the flying field, which was actually a local racetrack. Fascinated, he watched the plane circle the track and then soar aloft, coming in a few minutes later for a perfect landing. He elbowed his way through the crowd and bombarded Grade with questions. Where had he learned to fly? How could Houdini learn? Where could be buy a plane? How much would it cost? Less than a week later, in November 1909, he purchased his own Voisin biplane.

Within a month, the showman had learned how to pilot the plane on his own. He charmed German Army officials into granting him permission to use their Hafaren parade grounds in nearby Wandsbek as a temporary airfield. Their only stipulation was that he teach the officers the mechanics of flight. Over the course of the next several weeks, he escaped from restraints by night and during the early daylight hours, he learned about flight from a French mechanic that he had hired named Brassac. Cold winter weather, high winds and occasional snow kept the plane on the ground, but Houdini patiently learned all there was to know about airplanes. Later, he kept his promise and passed on his newly learned techniques to the cooperative German officers.

When the weather finally cleared, a confident Houdini took his place behind the controls of his flying machine. Brassac spun the propeller and the biplane smoothly lifted from the field. The flight was a short one. "I smashed the machine. Broke propeller all to hell," the rookie airman wrote in his diary that night. Houdini was unhurt and the damage to the machine was slight, although it took nearly two weeks for him to get replacement parts from France. Brassac managed to put it all back together.

Houdini's new Voisin plane. He learned to master it in Germany

Houdini made his first successful flight on November 26, 1909 over the Hufaren parade grounds. A photographer recorded the event for posterity. During the rest of his engagement at the Hansa, which closed at the end of December, Harry spent all of his spare time with his flying machine.

Houdini made his first flight on November 26, 1909 above a German Army air field.

Harry's plane was crated up and shipped to Australia. The crates arrived without any damage.

Houdini sailed for Australia on January 7, 1910. Stored in the hull of the ship was Houdini's crated Voisin biplane, as well as an extra motor and numerous spare parts. Brassac, his mechanic, shared a cabin with Franz Kukol, his assistant.

Houdini was appearing at the New Opera House in Melbourne and, as usual, planned a spectacular stunt to publicize the show. On February 18, more than twenty thousand people lined the Queen's Bridge and the banks of the Yarra River to see the manacled escapologist plunge into the murky waters below.

A much smaller crowd was present less than a month later at Digger's Rest, a field just outside of the city, when Houdini flew the first plane on the continent. Eager to take advantage of some good flying weather, Houdini went to the field after his show and slept in the tent that served as a hangar for his biplane. On March 16, at 5:00 a.m., Houdini's plane was wheeled out on the wooden planks that served as a take-off area. He donned a pair of goggles and a cap and climbed behind the steering wheel. With a wave to Bess, the propeller was started, the mooring line was cast off and the

Houdini strikes a pose next to his Voisin biplane.

Houdini became the first man to fly in Australia on March 16, 1910

engine began to roar. The plane shot forward and up, soaring gracefully into the morning sky. Houdini circled the field and then headed back toward the runway. As the plane touched down, the assembled audience clapped and laughed with approval. Houdini came in for a perfect landing after the first sustained flight in Australian history.

Houdini made a number of other flights but on April 20, the Voisin was struck by a crosswind and fell rapidly, hitting the ground with a heavy thud. The jagged ground caused one of the landing wheels to snap and break. Harry was unhurt but the plane sustained fairly serious damage.

That same night at the Tivoli Theater, three asylum attendants tied Houdini with linen bandages, rolled him like a mummy in sheets, then strapped him to an iron hospital bed frame. Buckets of water were tossed on the sheets to tighten them and make release even more difficult.

Harry began his struggle to escape by attempting to free his feet, kicking, turning and twisting. He managed to slip his left hand free from the bonds. More footwork distracted the observers as he released his right hand. He squirmed his way an inch at a time until his head reached the railing at the end of the bed. He called to Franz Kukol, who wiped the perspiration from his face with a handkerchief, the carefully tilted a glass of water for Harry to drink from.

As soon as his brief rest period was over, he started over again, rolling his legs from side to side, then kicking upward until his feet were free of the sheets. A cheer went up from the audience. He now squirmed into a sitting position and vigorous twisting and pulling released his arms, as well as his hands.

It seemed that he was now almost completely free, but there were still bandages tied around his knees, thighs and chest. Finally, straining against the cloth strips, he pulled his legs out, then his midsection, then he pulled his head through the bandage around his chest. Free of the cloth strips tied to the bed, he was still wound in wet sheets. He dropped from the bed to the floor. One of the men who had challenged him to make the escape bent down to help him unwind from the sheets, but Harry warned him away. With a mighty effort, he suddenly rolled across the stage and jumped to his feet, completely free.

Only a man in excellent physical condition, with complete control of his muscles and careful concentration, could have beaten the challenge. It took thirty-seven minutes of strain and tension, with only a brief pause for a sip of water, to do what seemed impossible.

The next morning, fresh and relaxed, he was back at the racetrack flying field, working with Brassac on the broken landing gear of his plane.

Australia's first aviator sailed for home on May 11. A day earlier, he had supervised the loading of his plane and props on board the ship. With the aerial triumph in Australia behind him, Harry lost the urge to pilot the plane himself, but his interest in aviation continued. He had planned to enter an air race when he returned to the United States, but he accepted vaudeville bookings that kept him out of the competition.

Houdini was in Chicago for the International Air Meet at Grant Park in August 1911. The air meet was a thrilling spectacle. Harry had the chance to meet famed flyers Orville Wright and Glenn Hammond Curtiss, who only seemed to know him as an Australian pilot and asked him all about his country.

Twenty-five planes were flown at the event. Five machines crashed on the first day, but none of the pilots were seriously injured. The tail of St. Croix Johnstone's plane was shattered, but the Chicagoan had mechanics at work on it just minutes after the crash. Lincoln Beachy, who once flew under the Suspension Bridge at Niagara Falls, was the show's star performer.

Two aviators fell into Lake Michigan on August 14 and a biplane burned to cinders when it struck a power cable the next day. Another flyer, William Baker, crashed on the lakeshore. St. Croix Johnstone, whose plane had been repaired, nosedived six hundred feet and was killed in Lake Michigan.

A benefit flying show, which raised $15,000, was staged for Johnstone's widow the day after the formal air meet ended. Houdini was the star of the show. With his hands and feet shackled, he jumped from a plane as it flew fifty feet above the lake, released himself under water and then swam up to the beach.

If Wright and Curtiss had no idea who Houdini was before the air meet -- they certainly knew who he was now.

"A SHOCK FROM WHICH I DO NOT THINK RECOVERY IS POSSIBLE"

While playing in England the following year, Houdini hired two more assistants, James Collins and James Vickery. Both men stayed with him for the rest of his life. Both men signed oaths to never reveal Houdini's secrets. Collins was an expert carpenter and metalworker and onstage, under Franz Kukol's direction, he was an efficient aide. Offstage, though, he was put to work on Harry's most pressing problem -- the construction of a feature escape to take the place of the Water Can.

Houdini was intrigued by the idea of an escape from a solid block of ice. As he designed the presentation, he would wear a diving suit and a helmet. He would be lowered into a tank with a glass front. A quick-freeze chemical solution would be poured in, over and around his body. Once solid ice was formed, the tank would be surrounded by a cloth-covered cabinet and Harry would free himself. He found that a diving helmet would hold a ten-minute supply of air, which was not a problem. Collins built a tank and for months, he tried unsuccessfully to mix a solution that would freeze the water quickly enough for a stage presentation. Houdini caught a severe cold during the tests and abandoned the experiment.

He soon devised another release. He was sealed in an oilskin bag, which was then enclosed in a rubber bag and lowered into a water-filled tank. A top was locked in place. Behind the cabinet's curtain, he freed himself and then emerged completely dry. The effect was good, but not as dramatic as Houdini hoped it would be.

Finally, in March, he developed the device that would take the place of the padlocked water can --- and lead to even more acclaim. When it was completed, the new "Chinese Water Torture Cell" was crated and stored until another blockbuster attraction was needed to bolster his act.

He continued to perform across England. In May, he attempted a double escape during a London show. He was nailed and roped in a box, which was lifted into a second, larger container. This was also nailed and roped as securely as the first. It took him twelve minutes to penetrate both.

In Leeds, a local brewer filled the Water Can with beer. Padlocked inside, Harry, who didn't drink, was overcome by the alcohol. Had it not been for quick thinking on the part of Franz Kukol, he might have drowned. He was semi-conscious when Kukol, disturbed by the silence from behind the curtain, dashed into the cabinet and pulled him out.

In London, he accepted a challenge to release himself from a "Rum Punch Hickory Barrel" at the Shepherd's Bush Empire Theater. He made sure the barrel was empty before he was locked inside.

When he returned to the United States in the fall of 1911, Houdini released himself after being tied to the plank by three sea captains. He also escaped from a deep-sea diving suit, even after the headpiece had been bolted to the shoulders. Then, he accepted his strangest challenge of all. A "sea monster," which looked something like a cross between a whale and a giant squid, had been found on a beach near Boston and the Lieutenant Governor of Massachusetts dared Houdini to "play Jonah." The manacled magician was forced through a slit in the embalmed carcass on the stage of a theater. Assistants "sewed" the opening closed with a metal chain, wound more chain around the carcass and then padlocked it. Working behind the cover of a curtain, Houdini freed himself in fifteen minutes. Afterward, he said that he would never try anything like it again; he had almost been overcome by the fumes of the embalming fluid that taxidermists had used inside of the creature.

In early November, as Harry had forced his way out of a challenge bag at the Temple Theater in Detroit, he had been injured internally. One of the round leather straps that had encircled the bag had been buckled with such pressure that it cause a blood vessel in his kidney to burst. He was unaware of the injury at the time and he bled for two weeks before he even considered going to a doctor. In Pittsburgh, a Mercy Hospital physician was shocked to learn that Harry had been continuing his strenuous performances without treatment.

Houdini grudgingly canceled a few weeks' worth of shows and returned to New York, where he endured his forced layoff. The doctor had told him that he had to rest until the injury healed and Bess and his mother tried to keep him in bed. Harry dictated replies to his piles of letters and correspondence, jotted down ideas for new escapes, leafed through old programs and posters in his ever-growing collection, and read scores of books that he had put aside for future study.

He was back on the road in December. He escaped from a tank of beer in Columbus, Ohio. Since his near-drowning in beer in England, Houdini had learned that he could put a coating of oil on his body to prevent the alcohol from penetrating his skin. In January 1912, in Philadelphia, the Bergdoll Brewing Company sent over eight gallons of lager to fill the specially designed water can. Later that month, in New York, Harry invited Jacob Ruppert, the challenger, to send over "eight to one hundred gallons" of Knickerbocker beer. The stagehands at the theater enjoyed the surplus.

In the summer of 1912, Harry came up with a new publicity feat for his run at Hammerstein's Roof Theater. A handbill was printed announcing that on Sunday, July 7, 1912, at 11:00 a.m., Houdini would be nailed in a box and thrown into the river. He would attempt to free himself while the box was submerged.

The New York Police, unlike those in other American cities, were uncooperative. They told Harry and the reporters and photographers who had assembled on Pier 6 on the East River that the stunt was off. So, Harry moved the feat to Governors Island, outside of the jurisdiction of the New York police. There, he was manacled and leg-ironed and put into a heavy packing case. His brother, Dr. Leopold Weiss, informed reporters that the box was twenty-four inches wide, thirty-

In New York, Houdini made one of his spectacular escapes from a sealed wooden box that was lowered into the water off Governors Island.

six high and thirty-four inches long. The lid was nailed in place, the box tied with ropes, and then encircled with steel bands. Two hundred pounds of iron were lashed to the sides of the case. The box, with Harry inside, was shoved down an incline and overboard. It plunged into the water and eleven seconds later, it lurched to one side, and then righted itself, with its top level with the water. Less than a minute later, Houdini appeared in the water fifteen feet away. He waved and swam to the boat. Two of his assistants and a longshoreman hauled him in. *Scientific American* magazine called it "One of the most remarkable tricks ever performed."

The stunt became so wildly popular that Harry had a huge tank built that held over five thousand gallons of water. It was installed on the stage of Hammerstein's theater and Houdini repeated the escape every night. Fifteen days later, he came up with an even more spectacular stunt. He was roped to the highest point of the Heidelberg Building tower at 42nd and Broadway at noon. Thousands watched from the street as he worked to free himself three hundred feet above their heads.

For Harry, though, the most memorable event of the two-month run at Hammerstein's was not one of his escapes, but an event that he staged solely for his mother. He arranged to be paid for his first week's salary in gold coins. Back home on West 113th Street, Harry told his mother to hold open her apron in her hands. He asked her if she remembered his promise to his father to look after her. She smiled and nodded her head. With a dramatic flourish, Houdini made the coins appear and they rained down into the apron.

Houdini: Among the Spirits - Page 50

By this time, Houdini was, at the age of thirty-eight, the best-known mystery performer in the world. He was soon to become even more widely known with the introduction of his "Chinese Water Torture Cell," which he was finally ready to take out of storage and put into production. It was first shown publicly during his engagement in Germany with the Circus Busch. The heavy metal-lined mahogany tank with a plate glass front could stand the most rigid examination. It was filled with water while the escapologist changed into his bathing suit.

A committee of volunteers was chosen prior to the show and they examined the tank, along with the cage that was to be lowered into the water-filled chamber. After they snapped the cuffs on his wrists, they also examined the heavy enclosures on his ankles and the massive frame that was fitted over them. Houdini was then hauled upward, turned upside down and lowered down into the water. Assistants locked the top of the tank and pushed a canopy over it. Houdini was visible through the plate glass on the front of

Harry introduced the Chinese Water Torture Cell into his act in 1912 and it remained a staple until the end of his career.

the tank until the drapes around it were closed. Two assistants stood by with axes; ready to break the glass in case of emergency. Suspenseful minutes passed and then Houdini parted the curtains to show-stopping applause. He would perform the Chinese Water Torture escape for the rest of his career.

Houdini returned home to the United States the following summer because he wanted to spend some time with his mother. Cecilia was now frail and weak and at the age of seventy-two, her health was failing. Harry played a single, month-long engagement at Hammerstein's Roof Theater, so that he could be close to her. She sat in the front row of the theater during the American debut of the new Chinese Water Torture Cell and led the applause for her favorite son.

The last time that he saw Cecilia was at his bon voyage party when he returned to Europe. He asked his mother what he should bring her home from Europe but she couldn't think of anything that she wanted or needed. To play along with his parting game, though, she said that she would like a pair of woolen slippers, size six. Back at her house, she observed the familiar ritual of winding the grandfather clock, which she never touched while her beloved Erich was home.

Harry's brother, Theo, took Cecilia for a vacation at Asbury Park, New Jersey when he opened there with his own show on July 14. The first day, he jumped from the end of the fishing pair and escaped from manacles and chains in the ocean. At the theater, he performed the old

Photographs Right & Left:
Houdini with his mother, who he adored.
Erich was always Cecilia's favorite son
and she missed him desperately when he
was traveling abroad. After her death,
Houdini did everything he could to try
and get in touch with her again, which
would eventually lead to his exposure of
fraudulent spirit mediums.

Houdini act, including challenge handcuff releases, the straitjacket, and the water can, all with his brother's blessing.

That night, at the Imperial Hotel, Cecilia was stricken with paralysis. Dr. James Ackerman said her condition was serious. Her entire body was affected and she was unable to speak. Theo telephoned his sister in New York and Gladys arrived the next morning. When Dr. Ackerman examined Cecilia again, he put her on the critical list.

Theo, performing as Hardeen, continued his shows at the Lyric Theater. On Wednesday night, July 16, he broke out of a challenge packing case, then hurried back to his mother's bedside. She tried to say something to him about Harry but she was unable to get the words out. She fell asleep. At fifteen minutes past midnight, Cecilia Weiss passed away.

Across the Atlantic, Houdini had opened at the Cirkus Beketow in Copenhagen. Two members of the royal family, Princes Aage and Axel, were in the audience. Harry delivered his stage patter in Danish and received a standing ovation.

At noon the following day, Thursday, July 17, Harry was being interviewed by newspapermen in the theater vestibule when a telegram arrived for him. Houdini ripped open the envelope and discovered that his beloved mother had died. He fell unconscious to the floor. A Danish physician was called in and examined the stricken magician. He prescribed immediate hospitalization but when Houdini objected, he insisted on a long period of rest. Beketow sympathetically released Harry from his Copenhagen contract and he canceled the rest of his European bookings and made plans to return to New York.

One thought was uppermost in Houdini's mind -- that he to see his mother before she was buried. He cabled Theo to delay the funeral and Houdini was able to book immediate passage on a ship that was sailing for New York. He remained under a doctor's care during the entire trip.

When he arrived in New York, he went straight to his mother's home. All of the furniture on

TO MY MOTHER.

"**MAMA!**"
The first sound all babies coo!
"Mother!"
The first word all babies speak!
"Mama!" Such a sacred word that, in all languages of the world, it is spelled and pronounced alike.

No matter what rank you hold, what wealth you possess, whether King or Queen, citizen or knave, but one Mother is the lot of each.

This Mother, to whom Eternity means no more than a fleeting, forgotten second of Time, when working or watching for her children, you must cherish while she is with you so that, when the pitiless Reaper brings from the Almighty the Mandate recalling Mother, you may receive from your ever-present Conscience the consolation coming from the knowledge that you tried to smooth, tried to remove, the briers from the path which she trod through this Mortal Valley of the shadow of Death.

The poet who wrote "God Himself could not be Everywhere so He made Mothers" - gives poetic utterance to my own sentiment.

HARRY HOUDINI.

the first floor had been rearranged for the funeral. Harry looked on his mother's face, then bent and pressed his ear to her chest. The heartbeat that had so reassured him as a small boy was now silent. In Bremen, Harry had recalled his mother's request from Europe and he had tearfully purchased her a pair of woolen slippers, size six. He now placed them at her side. Some time late in the night, he stopped the grandfather clock that Cecilia always wound while he was away. Houdini later said that he felt that his life had stopped too.

After the funeral, Harry visited the cemetery daily. Some times in the dark hours of the night, Bess would hear him call his mother's name. During the day, he read and re-read the letters that Cecilia had written to him over the years. Later, he had them translated into English so that he could read them more effortlessly. It was the only way that he had to keep a little part of her alive.

Cecilia's death was the greatest blow that Harry ever suffered. He often said that the death of his mother had been "a shock from which I do not think recovery is possible."

It was not until September that Houdini could force himself back to work. He opened at the Apollo Theater in Nuremberg. He was still in mourning. His stationary carried a wide black border and many of his shows were carried out almost as routine. It would be weeks before he began to recover from his grief and as he did, his old desire to produce a big magic show returned.

A supper was held at the Magician's Club in his honor and during a short speech, Houdini spoke about his mother: "My mother was everything to me. It seemed like the end of the world when she was taken from me. Not until she lay dying did I realize how inexpressibly futile is a man's intelligence and determination when face-to-face with death. When her last hour came, I thought mine would soon follow. Everything seemed turned to dust and ashes for me. All desire for fame and fortune had gone from me. I was alone with my bitter agony. But time, the great healer, has brought me some measure of solace."

In mid-April, the "king of escapologists" coined himself a new title. He arranged with the theater managers who booked his Water Cell act for special all-magic performances during the week. For these special occasions, typical handbills were printed that read:

The World Famous Self-Liberator
HOUDINI
The Supreme Ruler of Magic will present a
GRAND MAGICAL REVUE
In which he will prove himself to be the Greatest Mystifier that
History Chronicles, introducing a number of problems from his inexhaustible
repertoire.
WHICH WILL BE SEEN FOR THE FIRST TIME ON ANY STAGE

Despite the bombastic billing, there was little new or amazing in the Houdini magical revue. He offered a vanishing assistant, coins that disappeared from his fingers and appeared in a glass box, standard illusions and a revival of the old "Metamorphosis" stunt. Bess, who hadn't appeared with Harry on stage since he had dropped it from the act, worked with him on this and other illusions.

In May, Houdini purchased a brilliant trick, "Walking through a Steel Wall," from London magician Sidney Josolyne. He decided to delay its initial presentation until his summer engagement at Hammerstein's in New York. He also purchased the "Expanding Cube," a small square that grew in size to reveal a girl beneath it, from Leah Goldston, wife of Will Goldston, a British magician and magic dealer. The cube was the final creation of Buatier De Kolta, an American magician who was a contemporary of Robert-Houdin. Houdini had presented this illusion in the last showing of his magic revue at the Empire Theater in Nottingham.

Despite the money and effort that went into it, the all-magic program was not a resounding success. Houdini was an adequate conjurer but his real skills were obvious in his escape acts. Bookers who saw the all-magic show urged Harry to concentrate on the Water Cell act, and other escapes, which was always salable for top dollar.

When Houdini went to pick up his tickets to return to America, he was told in confidence that Theodore Roosevelt would be on the same ship. Harry took a taxi to the *Telegraph* newspaper office. The paper had started a series by the former president on his South American expedition. In a few minutes, with the help of a reporter friend, he had a copy of a Roosevelt map, as yet unpublished, and other facts that were unknown to the public.

During a shipboard performance given by Houdini, he asked the spectators to write down questions on slips of paper. As Roosevelt wrote, he was advised to turn his back so that Harry couldn't decipher the words by watching the motion of the top of his pencil. Roosevelt then folded the paper and dropped it between two blank slates, which Houdini tied together. After Harry asked for "spirit aid," the slates were parted to reveal a chalked map with an arrow indicating a point by the River of Doubt on one of them. The other slate now carried the words "near the Andes" and the signature of W.T. Stead, the British spiritualist who had gone down aboard the Titanic two years earlier.

Houdini with Theodore Roosevelt

Roosevelt was astonished. The question that he had written on his paper had been, "Where was I last Christmas?" and Harry's answer had been correct. The radio operator on board the ship sent the story ahead to New York and it became a minor sensation.

In July, Houdini opened his third summer season at the Hammerstein's Roof Theater. Two escapes from submerged boxes in the East River announced the news to New Yorkers that he was back in town. He began his third week at the theater with "Walking Through a Brick Wall." This was actually Josolyne's steel wall stunt but Harry felt that it would be more effective with audiences if they could actually see a brick wall constructed on stage. Twice daily, bricklayers built a wall nine feel high in a steel frame that was mounted on a wheeled base. To allay suspicions that a trapdoor might be used, a rug was spread on the stage and a large square of muslin was placed over it. The wall, inspected by a committee of audience members, was then rolled into position at the center of the muslin, with one end turned toward the crowd. Houdini, in a long white coat, stood to the left of the wall. A six-foot-high, threefold screen closed him in. The audience could see the bricks above and to the sides of the screen. Another screen was

placed on the other side of the wall.

As he prepared to walk through, Harry raised his hands above the screen and waved them about. He shouted, "Here I am!" As the hands vanished from view, he called out, "Now I'm gone." The screen was pulled away and Houdini was nowhere to be seen. When the other screen was opened, Harry was standing there, smiling enigmatically.

The stunt was performed over and over again, once with thirty spectators surrounding the structure, leaving only the front unobstructed so that the audience could have a clear view. The *Sunday World* Magazine devoted a full page to the puzzling feat -- which still amazes audience to this day.

Houdini was working in the United States when the Great War broke out in 1914. Since the European theaters were closed to him for the duration, he perfected a new publicity stunt to bring in the crowds to American theaters --- a straitjacket escape made while dangling high in the air, upside down and suspended from the top of a building. More than twenty thousand people turned out to watch him wriggle out of his bindings in Providence, Rhode Island. Another fifty thousand turned out in Baltimore and twice that many gathered in the nation's capital. Houdini ended the stunt by letting the straitjacket fall a dozen stories or more to the street below. Then, he extended his arms and took a bow while still hanging in mid-air.

In August, before going back on the road, Houdini entertained the prisoners at Sing Sing, the first important magician to perform behind the penitentiary's walls since Alexander Herrmann in 1896. Houdini kept the convicts' attention for three solid hours. Films were shown of his miraculous escapes. Playing cards rose from an isolated pack at his command. A rabbit appeared from an empty box. There was an unexpected reaction when Harry borrowed a watch and conjured it into the center of a loaf of bread. Houdini later wrote, "When I broke the loaf in half, two convicts grabbed the bread and ate it. It was white bread and I think they only get gray or black... Next time I'll produce it in the midst of a pound cake."

Never had he had a more completely enthralled

audience. Every motion of his handcuff, straitjacket and wooden crate escape was carefully observed. His methods inspired at least one convict, sentenced to life in prison, to make a successful jail break a few weeks later.

On June 12, 1917, two months after the United States declared war on Germany, Houdini registered for the draft. At the age of 43, he likely knew that he would not be inducted but he used the opportunity to offer his services performing at training camps, in Red Cross shows, and staged his straitjacket escape high above Broadway as members of the Society of American Magicians and their wives sold war bonds in the street. Houdini had recently been elected president of the prestigious society and, under his leadership, new affiliates were being formed all over the country.

He had tried, when he played the Palace Theater a year earlier, to get permission from Police Inspector Thomas V. Underhill to stage his straitjacket escape over Broadway. The request had been refused but now Elsa Maxwell, the gossip columnist, author, songwriter and soon to be known as America's most famous hostess, secured a permit for him. The Society of American Magicians gave her a gold medal in appreciation. Handbills for a fund-raising event were passed out to the thousands of people who lined the streets to see Houdini's traffic-stopping stunt.

Houdini's persuasive powers managed to bring Harry Kellar, the dean of American magicians, out of retirement in Los Angeles to make a "farewell appearance" at the benefit show. The evening began with seven magicians working side by side on the stage. For a finish to their act, they produced a red banner with S.A.M. (the initials for the Society of American Magicians) on it in gold letters. They strung it from man to man and departed from the stage.

Raymond Hitchcock, a musical comedian, offered a burlesque conjuring act. Other magicians rolled up their sleeves before they worked their tricks. Hitchcock rolled up his trouser legs. Arnold de Biere, a noted magician, acted as his assistant. Julius Zancig and his wife Agnes sent and received thoughts. Takasi produced his Oriental assistant from an empty sedan chair, linked and unlinked steel rings, and tore and restored tissue paper.

Then, Houdini took the spotlight. He was there, he said, to introduce America's greatest illusionist, who had made the trip from California to aid in a cause that was close to his heart. It was a moment of great humility for Harry, who was used to promoting his own name rather than that of someone else. The crowd called out a deafening welcome to the tall, bald, sun-tanned Kellar. A table floated in the air when the aging magician touched it with his fingertips. He was tied into a cabinet, from which he produced "spirit" phenomena. The great artist conjured up an amazing night of magical memories from days gone by.

After his final illusion, Kellar took a deep bow and turned to leave the stage. The applause literally shook the theater and Houdini stopped him from leaving. He signaled the crowd to be silent. He could not allow Kellar to simply walk off the stage after his final performance. Members of the society emerged from the wings with a sedan chair and Kellar sat down on the cushioned seat. The chair was shouldered by magicians and paraded around the stage as he was showered with flowers. The audience stood, joined hands and sang "Auld Lang Syne" as Kellar, with a final wave of his hand, was taken off into the shadows of backstage.

Left: One of Harry Kellar's classic posters from his performing days. Houdini often referred to him as one of America's greatest magicians.

Right: Houdini visited with Kellar in California, where the elderly magician was enjoying his retirement.

There was still more show to come. Houdini performed his trunk illusion and the Water Cell escape. Louise Homer sang "The Star-Spangled Banner." A detachment of French sailors drilled with the red, white and blue flags of the two nations but the evening finally reached its peak when Kellar returned to the stage one last time to take a final bow.

Charles Dillingham, the producer at the Hippodrome, was so impressed by Houdini's staging of the affair that he asked him to create something spectacular at the theater in the months ahead. He had no idea at the time that Houdini would be creating what was perhaps the greatest illusion of his career.

On January 7, 1918, Houdini introduced the biggest illusion ever staged at the New York Hippodrome --- or perhaps anywhere else. He called it the "Vanishing Elephant" and for this trick, he obtained the services of Jennie, a ten thousand-pound elephant who was placed inside a wooden box that was roughly the size of a small garage. Other magicians vanished doves and rabbits and sometimes even horses and donkeys, but no one before Houdini dared to attempt the disappearance of an elephant. Harry's friend, Charles Morritt, baffled audiences in England with a "Disappearing Donkey" and he was the one who originally conceived of the idea. When he described it to Houdini, Harry immediately bought the exclusive worldwide performing rights.

Once Jennie was inside the box with her trainer, Harry fired a pistol. His assistants opened the front curtains and removed a circular section at the back of the box to allow the audience to see through the stage curtains at the rear --- the elephant was gone! Curiously, no one seemed to notice that the trainer vanished along with the elephant.

"With this baffling mystery," wrote Sime Silverman, the editor of *Variety*, "Houdini puts his title of escape artist behind him and becomes the Master Magician."

Hippodrome patrons knew the animal could not have gone through a trapdoor. Beneath the stage was the famous Hippodrome pool. Later in the show, Houdini escaped from a box that was lowered into the water. A critic from the *Brooklyn Eagle* noted: "The program says that the elephant vanished into thin air. The trick is performed fifteen feet from the backdrop and the cabinet is slightly elevated. That explanation is as good as any."

Some magicians said that the elephant vanish wasn't much of a trick, but when pressed to explain it, none of them could. Three illusionists announced that they would have their own disappearing elephants the next season. One, Harry Blackstone, claimed that he had invented the illusion but could not offer a shred of evidence to prove it.

Houdini had been booked for six weeks at the theater with this illusion but the impact of the stunt prolonged the engagement to nineteen weeks, the longest theater engagement of his career.

There was no question about it --- Houdini had finally arrived.

Houdini and Jennie the Elephant, who he caused to disappear at the Hippodrome during what was called "the biggest illusion ever staged!"

HOUDINI AT THE MOVIES

His career had reached the level that he had always dreamed of, but Harry was as troubled as he was famous. He was still depressed over the death of his mother and soon became obsessed with it. After she died, he was observed many times at the cemetery where she was buried, lying face down on her grave and holding long conversations with her. He felt that he had to communicate with her and that was when he turned to Spiritualism.

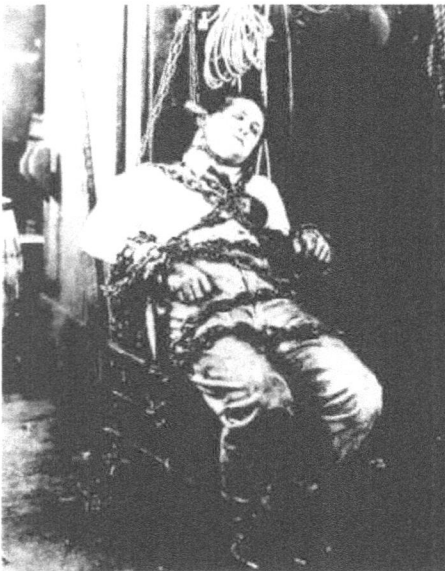

Houdini in a scene from *The Master Mystery*

But Houdini, having conducted fake séances during a low time in his career, soon discovered that the mediums he visited were trying to pass off cheap magic tricks as the work of spirits. He knew he could duplicate their methods on stage and it was not long before his efforts to reach his mother became secondary to his need to expose the frauds. He quickly became very bitter and willing to believe that all mediums were fakes. He began investigating their methods and claims and later became a self-appointed crusader against them.

Meanwhile, his career continued to soar. Before he closed at the Hippodrome, the magician signed a contract with B.F. Rolfe of Octagon Films to star in a movie serial called *The Master Mystery*. Houdini would play Quentin Locke, an undercover agent for the Justice Department, who used his expertise as an escape artist to thwart the efforts of the villain of the serial. In different scenes, Houdini's character was buried alive in

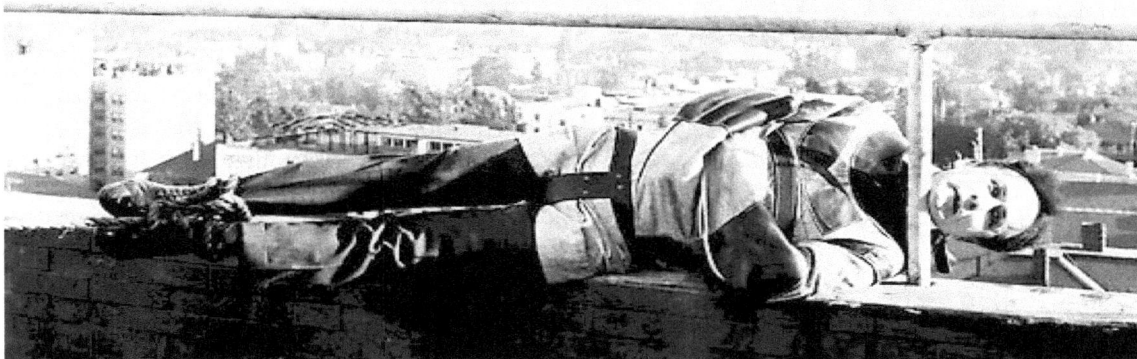

a gravel pit, tied in the bottom of an elevator shaft as the car was lowered to crush him, suspended upside down over boiling acid, and even strapped into an electric chair. Somehow, though, he always survived. Houdini broke three bones in his left wrist while filming one of the early scenes but production continued. He had to wear a leather wrist support when he returned to perform at the Hippodrome in August. In spite of this, he managed all of his escapes and illusions without a hitch.

Houdini made his first Hollywood feature film, *The Grim Game*, for Paramount Pictures in the spring of 1919. The story of the film was designed to present the escape artist at his daredevil best. He broke out of a jail cell, climbed the outside of a building to reach a dangling rope, and used it to slide to the street. Captured after a fight, Houdini was taken to a rooftop, strapped in a straitjacket and suspended upside down over the side. He released himself, fell into an awning, and dropped to the ground. Moments later, he rolled under the wheels of a moving truck, grasped the underside and rode away beneath it. Later, he was caught in a rope-sling bear trap and tossed into a well.

The screenplay also called for Harry to make a plane-to-plane transfer in mid-air -- but things didn't exactly ago according to the script. As the two aircraft maneuvered into position, they collided, became locked together and spiraled to the earth. Director Irvin Willat, in a third plane, kept his camera running. The two flying machines managed to separate before they crashed in a bean field. Miraculously, no one was seriously injured. The story line of the film was changed to include the footage of the accident in the film.

Filming *The Grim Game*

One of Houdini's best-kept secrets was that he was not involved in the crash. His left arm was in a

JESSE L. LASKY
PRESENTS

HOUDINI
IN
"THE GRIM GAME"

BY ARTHUR B. REEVE AND JOHN W. GRAY
DIRECTED BY IRVIN WILLAT

A PARAMOUNT-ARTCRAFT PICTURE

sling at the time. He had fallen a mere three feet during the jail escape sequence and fractured his wrist again. A double was used for the plane-to-plane switch and other doubles were used during for the more hazardous feats in the movie. The other doubles were dummies with painted faces dressed in striped shirts and dark trousers to match the clothes that Harry wore. The dummies were filmed in long shots, then studio close-ups of the star were inserted to create the illusion that he performed breathtaking escapes that even Houdini himself would not risk.

After *The Grim Game* was completed, Harry returned to New York to take over the management of Martinka's magic shop, which had been purchased by Houdini's friend Charles J. Carter in 1917. He had formed a company to purchase it from his friend before he went to Hollywood. While he was in New York, *The Grim Game* opened at the Broadway Theater. The publicity campaign featured the plane accident in mid-air. Houdini offered $1,000 to anyone who could prove the collision had been faked. Like all Houdini challenges, it was a safe bet to make.

Harry barely had time to go through the stock of Martinka's and put aside choice pieces for his personal collection before returning to Hollywood to star in another Jesse Lasky picture. The filming of Terror Island began in September. The new film followed the old formula of fast action, wild escapes and spectacular stunts.

Motion pictures had become, as aviation had been years before, Houdini's major obsession. He sold his share of the magic shop and started a film-developing corporation, which lost large amounts of money. Houdini persuaded his brother Theo to leave the road and manage it, but this was not enough. Harry Kellar, an investor in the company, advised Harry to give it up but he wouldn't listen. He used a good portion of his income trying to keep the business afloat.

With new responsibilities came a need to make more money. It had been six years since Houdini had toured in England and theater managers were now asking him to honor contracts that had been postponed by the war. *The Master Mystery* had been a success in Britain and new demand had risen for his act. This time, he would not only be a vaudeville headliner, but an

American movie star making personal appearances. He sailed for England in late December 1919.

While working in England, Harry's friend Will Goldston suggested that he put together an outline for a book, *Magical Ties and Escapes*. Another project, which took more of his time, was research for a history on Spiritualism. In the aftermath of the war, the interest in the movement had grown. The British press reported that such noted figures as Sir Arthur Conan Doyle were firm believers in Spiritualism. Houdini could not understand how Doyle, who had shown such keen powers of reasoning and deduction in his Sherlock Holmes stories, could be deceived by simple tricks in dark séance rooms. At the same time, he was appalled by the cold-hearted nature of those professional mediums who took advantage of grief-stricken mothers and widows who flocked to séances in the hope that they might talk with their lost sons and husbands. He began attending as many as two séances each day, gathering material for his book, studying the methods of fraudulent mediums --- and perhaps still hoping to see some bit of reality in the Spiritualists' attempts to contact the dead.

Houdini visited more than one hundred mediums during his British tour. Despite his self-proclaimed open mind, he found no evidence that communication with the dead was anything other than self-deception or purposeful trickery. "The more I investigate," Houdini wrote, "the less I can make myself believe."

In March, Harry injured his right ankle while escaping from the Water Torture Cell. During his doctor-ordered week of recuperation, he put his Spiritualism notes in order. He felt there was a pressing need for a debunking book on spirit phenomena and he used his voyage home to America to begin work on it.

He had no idea that his research into the supernatural would not only change his life and career but would violently end a friendship that was only just beginning.

THE HAUNTED FRIENDSHIP

While touring in England in 1920, Houdini met a man with whom he would maintain a rather strange friendship over the course of the next two years. He was the famous author Sir Arthur Conan Doyle and the two of them met in England and began a good natured but antagonistic relationship. Doyle believed that Spiritualism was of great importance to the world, while Houdini actively campaigned against it and its "mediumistic parlor tricks." The two men, both of whom possessed a vast knowledge of the movement, argued long and inconclusively but remained close until a series of incidents caused the friendship to abruptly end. A rift developed between them and was never repaired, resulting in both public and private battles between the pair until Houdini's death in 1926.

Conan Doyle & Houdini

Arthur Conan Doyle was born in Edinburgh, Scotland, on May 22, 1859. He was the eldest son of Charles Altamont Doyle, an assistant surveyor in the Scottish Office of Works, and Mary Foley, an Irish Catholic woman whose mother was Charles Doyle's landlady. Charles Doyle supplemented his earnings from his civil service job with money he made from painting and illustrating books. Success eluded him and biographies of his son described him as a dreamy aesthetic figure. Suffering from alcoholism and epilepsy, he left his job while in his forties and spent most of the remainder of his life in nursing homes for alcoholics and mental asylums. Doyle's mother, Mary, was the backbone of the family. She was a well-read woman and a great storyteller. Years later, Arthur would credit her for his love of literature. She bore her husband ten children in all. Five girls and two boys survived into adulthood.

Growing up, Doyle spent two years at Hodder, a Jesuit-run preparatory school and then when he was eleven he moved to Stonyhurst public school, another Jesuit institution. He had been allowed to attend Stonyhurst at no charge because it was hoped that he might dedicate his life to the church. At Stoneyhurst he was remembered for his untidiness and his insistence on getting his own way. As a result, he spent a great deal of time in the headmaster's office. He eventually became disenchanted with Catholicism and decided to pursue a medical career instead. Over the next few years, Doyle endured the spartan conditions of boarding school, the corporal punishment and the poor food. He excelled at sports, especially cricket, and at sixteen he passed his graduate exam with honors. Doyle began working hard to obtain a scholarship for his medical studies and although he was awarded one, a series of official mistakes prevented him from receiving it. His family could not afford to send him to school, so he worked a series of jobs and attended medical college at the same time. He completed his schooling in Edinburgh in 1881 with a Masters in biology.

Sir Arthur Conan Doyle

Doyle was eager to start a medical practice after graduation and had also developed a love for writing. He hoped to supplement his practice by selling short stories to the magazines of the day but while in school, he recognized the importance of working first and writing later. He wrote and sold a short story or two and then, as a third-year student, he signed on as a ship's surgeon for a whaler that was making a seven-month voyage to the Arctic. Doyle got along well with the ships' crew. He was by now a massive and strong young man, an all-around sportsman and a man of incredible strength. His boxing skills also served him well and he won a bout with the ship's steward on the first night out of port.

The trip to the Arctic so fulfilled his taste for action and adventure that he signed on to another ship the following year. This time, he was a ship's surgeon on a voyage taking cargo and crew down the west coast of Africa. This adventure was far less enjoyable and he became extremely ill, likely with malaria. He came home with a small amount of money and decided to start his medical practice. Doyle went to work in a small village outside of Plymouth called Southsea, where he practiced for eight years.

While working as a poor doctor in Southsea, Doyle tried to make a name for himself as a writer.

He made little money during this period of his life but he managed to supplement his meager income by selling adventure stories. His London relatives offered to send him their ailing friends as patients, on the condition that he practiced Catholicism. He refused, declaring himself an agnostic. As he settled into his practice, he wrote as often as time allowed and since he had few patients, he would often spend hours scratching out action-packed stories as his desk. In 1886, he penned his first Sherlock Holmes mystery but had difficulty finding anyone to publish it. He eventually sold it outright for a small sum. The publishers told him that at the time, they didn't plan to publish it for at least a year "as the market is flooded at present by cheap fiction."

The story, called "A Study in Scarlet," appeared in the *Beeton's Christmas Annual* for 1887 and met with success but Doyle had no interest in being merely a writer of short detective stories. Instead, he began research and wrote a lengthy historical novel called *Micah Clarke*. The book appeared in 1889 and was another immediate success. Six more stories about Sherlock Homes followed in the recently founded *Strand Magazine* and an American publisher requested a Holmes novel, spurring Doyle to write "The Sign of the Four." Doyle meant to write only those stories about Sherlock Holmes and no more. He thought of himself as a serious novelist and the Holmes stories were merely a distraction to him. However, when the publishers offered more and more money for additional tales, Doyle surrendered --- and the Sherlock Holmes saga began.

Before Sherlock Homes was a sensation in England, though, Doyle was already busy writing another historical novel, *The White Company* (which he considered his best work) and attending to his practice. His younger brother, Innes, had come to live with him in Southsea and he assisted Doyle in his work. He still saw his writing as simply an added income to his position as a doctor.

In 1885, Doyle married Louise Hawkins, the older sister of a patient of his who had died. She was a sweet and docile woman who remained in the background, perhaps overshadowed by her larger-than-life spouse. In 1889, their daughter Mary was born. In 1890, a strange event occurred that may have only been a coincidence but in later years, many would wonder. Not long after Mary's birth, Doyle received word of a demonstration that was taking place in Berlin by a doctor who claimed to be able to cure tuberculosis, which at the time was called consumption. Doyle became obsessed with attending the conference, even though he did not specialize in treating consumption. He went to Berlin but unfortunately, the trip turned out to be fruitless for he arrived too late to attend the presentation. Doyle's interest in the lecture was never fully explained but tragically, three years later, his beloved Louise was diagnosed with consumption was given only a few months to live. Was it merely a coincidence or was Doyle's keen interest in the subject matter, as some have suggested, a foreshadowing of things to come?

A chance meeting with a physician in London convinced Doyle to move his practice to the city. He decided to specialize in eye care but to do so he needed to attend a six-month training session in Vienna. The Southsea practice was abandoned, Mary was sent to her grandmother and Doyle and Louise set off for Austria. The entire trip turned out to be a disaster. The lectures were given in German and while Doyle had a conversational knowledge of the language, he was unable to follow the technical terms. He wrote a short book "The Doings of Raffles Haw," instead and he and Louise left Vienna after two months instead of six. When the couple returned to England, Doyle set up practice in London in Devonshire Place, at the top of Wimpole Street. It was a quiet

Conan Doyle's first wife, Louise Hawkins

and ideal location -- for writing anyway -- for not a single patient darkened Doyle's doorstep. He spent all of his time writing and it was here that he created the next set of Sherlock Holmes tales. The immediate success of the stories, the lack of patients and a severe bout with influenza that nearly killed him made his next decision an easy one. He would give up his medical work and turn all his attentions to writing.

Sherlock Holmes was based on Edgar Allen Poe's detective C. Auguste Duphin and Eugene Francois Vidoq, a former criminal who became chief of the Paris police force. Physically, Holmes resembled Dr. Joseph Bell, one of Doyle's teachers at the University of Edinburgh. His surname came from Oliver Wendell Holmes, an American physician and poet whom Doyle greatly admired and father of the Supreme Court justice by the same name.

Conan Doyle was in his early thirties when he decided to break with medicine and over the next ten years, he became increasingly more successful and increasingly more of a public figure. He emerged into the last decade of the nineteenth century as one of the most influential characters of his generation. To one segment of the public, he was the creator of Sherlock Holmes, while to another he was the author of historical novels and adventure stories. To another, even those who were not interested in his gripping tales, he was a man of total faith in the imperial destiny of Britain and a personage who was ready and eager to play a role in public affairs.

Doyle was a figure that most men aspired to imitate. He looked more like a sportsman than a man of letters, was a robust outdoorsman and an avid boxer, adept at soccer and cricket. He was also, like many men and women of his generation, concerned about religion. He lost his Catholic faith while still a young man and for a time was mildly agnostic. While living in Southsea, he became interested in psychical research and began reading heavily on the subject.

He also had the opportunity to visit séances and attend experiments in telepathy and thought transference. His search for answers led to a meeting with Sir Oliver Lodge, one of the leading paranormal investigators of the time, and in 1893, he joined the Society for Psychical Research. He watched with interest the public's fascination with Spiritualism but did not understand how ghostly phenomena warranted a faith and religion based around it, at least not yet. He did become more and more interested in the Spiritualist movement although, at first, his interested was tinged heavily with skepticism.

Sadly, Doyle's personal life was not as successful as his professional one. He refused to accept the diagnosis that doctors had given to Louise and became determined to find a cure for her tuberculosis. According to the doctors, she only had a few months left but Doyle was sure that he could prolong her life. He set aside his career and began taking Louis to various places that had been recommended as being helpful to patients suffering from consumption. He traveled first to Switzerland and then was told by a friend and fellow writer, Grant Allen, who also suffered from tuberculosis, that he had found the climate in the English county of Sussex, south of London, to be of great benefit. Doyle purchased an imposing red brick home there called Undershaw in the village of Hindhead. The house was one of the first in the region to have electric lighting. This was Louise's home until her death in 1906.

The strain of caring for Louise took its toll on not only Doyle's own peace of mind but on his relationship with his children, as well. A son, Kingsley, had been born in 1892 and to he and Mary their father was a lovable but slightly fearsome character. He could be reckless and boyish with them one moment and then, when tired or worried, curt and sharp with them the next. Much of his strain undoubtedly came after 1897, when he met a young woman named Jean Leckie. If one needed any evidence to prove that Doyle was an honorable and respectable man, they need only examine the fact that his relations with Jean, who was fourteen years his junior, remained platonic until after Louise died. A year later, they married and she bore him three more children. Some of his friends were critical of his attachment to Jean but as far as Doyle was concerned, the relationship remained innocent for a number of years.

Jean Leckie, who became Doyle's second wife in 1906

Doyle's grief over the sad state of affairs at home, as well as his mixed emotions about Jean, led him to escape into his writing and into the bright lights of public life. He attended dinners, joined literary societies, went on trips and even wrote a stage play called "Waterloo," which was performed by the eminent actor Henry Irving. He took his brother Innes, who was about to enter the military, to the United States, where he went on a book tour, giving talks and readings. He became very popular with Americans, who loved his bluff manner, his cheerfulness, his Scottish accent and his simple and unpretentious ways. Doyle found the wide-open spaces and outdoor life of the United States to be invigorating and felt very much at home. Since Americans loved the Sherlock Holmes stories as much as the British did, Conan Doyle was probably the best-known Englishman in the U.S. for many years.

While visiting fellow Englishman Rudyard Kipling at his home near Brattleboro, Vermont, Doyle gave the author of *The Jungle Book* and *Gunga Din* a few pointers at golf, "While the New England rustics watched us from afar, wondering what on earth we were at."

During the Boer War, Doyle came into his own as an adventurous public figure. The war began in October 1899 and just before Christmas of that year, in what was known as Black Week, the British military suffered three staggering defeats at the hands of an army of farmers in South Africa. There was much alarm in Britain, together with a patriotic upsurge, and on Christmas Eve, Doyle decided to volunteer for South Africa. His mother was angry and distressed, believing that his life was of more value to his country at home. There were thousands who could fight, she told him, but only one who could have created Sherlock Holmes (Doyle's mother never understood her son's disinterest in the great detective and was very angry when he killed him off by having him plummet over Reichenbach Falls during a fight with his archenemy, Professor Moriarty). She also believed that Doyle's sympathies were better aimed at the Boers that at the wealthy companies who were using the military to protect their interests in the African nation.

Many in England shared her feelings about the Boers. The discovery of gold in the Witwaterstrand region of South Africa in the 1880s had led many seeking a quick fortune to descend on Johannesburg. Cecil Rhodes was the operator of many commercial endeavors who used the British "Imperial ideals" as an excuse to run roughshod over the people of the area. Conan Doyle himself admired and respected the Boers, but his adherence to Britain and the Empire was unquestioning. He decided to enlist but the army had little use for a forty-year-old recruit and placed him on a waiting list. When the chance came for him to join a hospital unit (at his own expense) that had been put together by his friend John Langman, he jumped at the chance. He became a doctor and an unofficial supervisor and shipped out to South Africa.

Doyle remained in South Africa for a little more than three months. After the capture of the Boer capital of Pretoria, the war (he thought) came to an end. He found the time he spent in the country to be deeply satisfying and after obtaining a number of first-hand accounts of the fighting, he wrote a book called "The Great Boer War" on his return to England. The book became very popular, although it was outdated by a subsequent history since what seemed to be the end of the war was not. It actually continued on as a guerilla conflict for nearly two years. Regardless, the book was successful and in the last chapter, Doyle suggested what he believed were some necessary military reforms. They caused a great stir and included the concealment of large guns (two batteries had almost been lost at one battle because a commander foolishly pushed them ahead of the infantry and provided no cover for them); the abandonment of cavalry swords and lances; and the development of a highly trained infantry that could be supplemented by national volunteer militia units. These ideas seem quite sensible today but shocked the army establishment of the time.

Doyle also found himself immersed in the controversy that surrounded the final months of the war. The guerilla war that continued brought a severe response from the British military. The

Boers were highly mobile, living off the land and moving around constantly, striking at British forces and then vanishing. The military established a series of blockhouses to try and contain the guerillas, burned their farms and built concentration camps for the women and children who were burned out. The camps were dirty and badly run and various epidemics like measles and typhoid continually swept through them. A number of articles and pamphlets appeared that described the conditions of the camps but which also made false claims about the conduct of British soldiers. They articles inflamed many European countries and Britain became widely criticized. In response, Doyle penned a small booklet called "The War in South Africa: Its Causes and Conduct" put together from eyewitness accounts in less than a week. He made a good case against the claims that British soldiers were raping Boer women and using dum-dum bullets that expanded on impact. He also admitted that while the camps had their shortcomings, they were necessary alternative to allowing the women and children to starve to death. The booklet had its effect, especially in other European countries, and managed to counter the anti-British sentiment. We would consider it to be propaganda today but it was done in support of a cause that the author truly believed in.

Before Doyle wrote the booklet, he had stood for Parliament in the 1900 general election. He was a Conservative candidate and while not in opposition to the Liberal policy of social reform at home, he joined the conservative Unionist party because they were pro-military and Empire. He ran for office in Edinburgh but had little chance of winning in the mostly Liberal area. His campaign was very effective, however. He spoke to workmen, gave informal speeches in the street and rented out an opera house for formal speeches in the evening. He ended up making fourteen appearances in less than three days, genially acknowledging the hecklers who called him "Sherlock Holmes" and focusing on the importance of military reforms, national defense and the Empire. Things looked well for him until, on election day, a fanatical Protestant hung posters throughout the district that proclaimed Conan Doyle to be a Jesuit-educated, Catholic agent --- a lie that must have galled a man who had long ago abandoned the Catholic faith. The posters likely swayed many voters but Doyle did improve the Unionist tally by fifteen hundred votes. Regardless, he lost the election. Years later, he admitted that he was glad that he had never ended up in politics. He would have never have been a good party man and he disliked electioneering. He was never that interested in politics but he was a fighter by nature and fighters never like to lose.

By this time, Doyle was not only a famous author but also a famous man and he was offered a knighthood, which he immediately refused, stating that a knighthood was a discredited title. His mother was furious and persisted with her demand that he reconsider until she eventually got her way. In 1902, he became Sir Arthur. Interestingly though, years later, in one of the last Sherlock Holmes stories, "The Adventure of the Three Garridebs," Dr. Watson mentions in passing that Holmes had refused a knighthood and named the year in which this occurred. Not surprisingly, it was 1902.

The Sherlock Holmes stories, along with his historical novels, made Conan Doyle a famous writer but it was his activities during the Boer War that made him a national celebrity. During the last ten years of the nineteenth century, he published five collections of short stories and eleven novels and would go on to write many more, including *The Lost World, The Hound of the Baskervilles* and others.

In 1911, Conan Doyle took part in a motorcar race called the Prince Henry Tour. He had long been fascinated with the automobile, having purchased his first in 1903 before he knew how to derive. He looked forward to a great sporting event. Prince Henry was Prussian and the race began in Germany and ended in London, after a circular tour of England and Scotland. It also pitted fifty British drivers against fifty German drivers and Conan Doyle drove his favorite motorcar, with Jean as his team member. A British team won the race and Prince Henry presented them with an ivory statuette called "Peace" but from what Doyle saw and heard during the race, he feared that war with Germany was not far off. He had been accompanied by various Prussian officers as observers and several of them made the assumption that war between the two nations was inevitable.

Doyle began preparing for war in the best way that he knew how --- with his pen. He told his brother Innes that he did not like the look of things and feared that England was not ready to fight. He exaggerated the effectiveness of the airship in those days but he was almost uncannily accurate about the threat posed by the new vessel, the submarine. He wrote a lengthy story called "Danger," in which Britain's enemy had a fleet of submarines that ignored the British Navy but made merciless attacks on merchant shipping, causing famine and forcing England to surrender. His warning about the submarine threat was mocked at the time it was written but three years later, the German naval secretary would write that Conan Doyle had been "the only prophet of the present form of economic warfare" as the Germans began preying on merchant vessels.

And while Conan Doyle was always an agent of reform and change when it came to politics and the military, he was not always so forward thinking with his ideas. He was a stoutly old-fashioned man and while embracing movements like Spiritualism in his later years, he was steadfastly opposed to others. He detested the women's suffrage movement and often spoke out against the actions of its radical members, calling them "wild women." The suffragettes responded by pouring sulfuric acid through the letterbox of Windlesham Manor, the home that Doyle had moved to in the East Sussex village of Crowborough, in 1909. Doyle's opposition to the suffragettes' cause was based on the belief that it was not only pointless for women to have the vote, but that it was unwomanly. On the other hand, he was sympathetic to the reform of the Divorce Law, by which a husband could gain a divorce on the grounds of his wife's adultery but a wife wishing a divorce had to prove not only adultery but brutality or desertion as well. He campaigned hard to get the law changed but this all was placed on the back burner when war was declared in August 1914.

Conan Doyle was again galvanized into action. He said after the fighting had ended that the Great War was the physical climax of his life, a remarkable statement considering that he was fifty-five years old at the time it started. Within a day or two, he had organized a Crowborough civilian group called the Volunteers. He received requests for their rules and methods from over twelve hundred other towns and villages, even though the volunteer force was disbanded by an order from the War Office a few weeks after it was founded. It was replaced by an official body

Conan Doyle in uniform during the war

that boasted more than two hundred thousand men. Doyle served in it as a private during the entire war. Most of the men were Sir Arthur's age or older but thought nothing of marching as many as fourteen miles each day, singing along the entire route.

He was invigorated by the war effort but it was not enough for him. He wanted to see action and volunteered for the Army. Needless to say, he was not accepted but he did send a flurry of ideas, many of them ingenious and practical, to the War Office. Since many of the military ships had few lifeboats, the sailors aboard board them had little chance of surviving if their ship sank or they fell overboard. Doyle suggested the idea of inflatable rubber rafts that could be used and while this idea was turned down, he did suggest the development of inflatable rubber collars for seamen to carry with them in their pockets. He also came up with an idea for soldiers to be fitted with body armor but it too was rejected.

Unfortunately, many of those who worked in the office agreed with his innovative notions but there was little they could do about it without approval from the high command. At the Ministry of Munitions, when he went there to argue for his body armor idea, he was told: "Sir Arthur, there is no use arguing here, for there is no one in this building who does not know that you are right!"

Ideas aside, his principal endeavor during the war was to rally Britain's spirits. Within a month of the war's beginning, he published a booklet called "To Arms" and quickly set to work on a history of the British campaign in France. He maintained contact with many of the British commanders and chronicled their efforts extensively, sometimes posting and receiving as many as five letters each day to and from the front. But he was not content to work from home. In 1916, he accepted an assignment to write about the Italian army and to visit the British front on the way. As a deputy-lieutenant of Surrey, he had the right to wear a uniform and his tailor "rigged me up in wondrous khaki garb which was something between that of a Colonel and a Brigadier, with silver roses instead of stars or crosses upon the shoulder straps." He looked especially impressive wearing his medals from South Africa, and was treated with respect everywhere he went. He went to France on a destroyer in the company of several generals and was allowed to meet up with Innes, who was now a Colonel.

His trip to the Italian front turned out to be a hazardous one. His hosts tried, without success, to keep him out of harm's way but the party was shelled and nearly hit and had to turn back. Doyle put together volumes of notes about the Italian troops, wrote them up on his return and was told that his trip was a great success. The expedition led to his having breakfast with Lloyd George, the new prime minister, and also to an invitation from the Australian government to see their section of the line. While on this trip, he saw part of the battle of St. Quentin. The end of the Great War must have brought mixed feelings to Doyle. He was undoubtedly overjoyed with the Allied victory but in another sense, his greatest adventure had come to an end. The marching and the drilling, the war correspondence, the dangerous journeys that took him into the heart of historical events all combined to indulge his boyish love of adventure.

But the war and its aftermath also brought him the deepest grief that he had ever known. First, his wife's brother and Doyle's friend, Malcolm Leckie, had been killed, along with two nephews and several other friends and relatives. And then Kingsley, the only son of his first marriage, and Doyle's beloved brother Innes, both died within a few weeks of one another. Kingsley had been badly wounded on the Somme and had died of pneumonia in October 1918. Not long after, Innes, now a brigadier general, also came down with pneumonia and died. Conan Doyle said and wrote very little about these deaths but they must have hit him quite hard, perhaps even harder than the death of his mother two years later.

Although these deaths were not responsible for his belief in Spiritualism, they surely must have had a great effect on the strength of his convictions. He had long been interested in the occult but at the beginning of the war had merely been sympathetic to the movement. The wartime deaths and the suffering that he witnessed must have convinced him of the need for spirits to live on. It was a time when the public at large felt a great urgency to turn toward spiritual things and as Spiritualism had seen a great revival following the Civil War, it would see another following World War I. The movement had just entered its modern heyday and standing at the forefront was Sir Arthur Conan Doyle.

Conan Doyle's interest in Spiritualism began when he was still an almost penniless young doctor living in Southsea. It was during a time when science was just starting to question the idea that another world might exist beyond our own and Doyle became caught up in the study, as well as in the burgeoning Spiritualist movement. He avidly followed the research that was being done and even attended a number of séances and kept detailed notes of what occurred there. Early in his research, he began to consider the idea that a great amount of the phenomena that he witnessed was genuine and that the knocks, raps, horn-blowing and messages from the dead were worthy of at least a cautious belief.

Somewhere along the line, his cautious skepticism gave way to outright acceptance. There has been much debate as to what finally immersed Doyle completely into the Spiritualist movement. Most believe that it was the series of

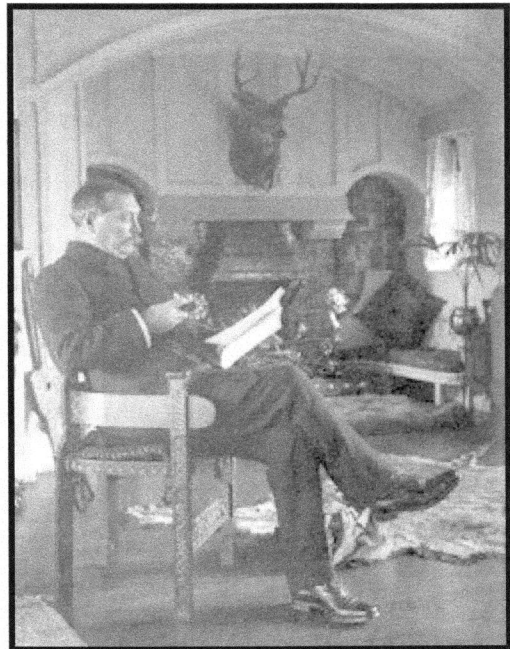

Conan Doyle in his study at Windlesham, his home in Crowborough, Sussex

deaths that occurred during the Great War that led Doyle to embrace the movement as he did. Soon after Kingsleys' death, he was convinced that he heard the voice of his son during a séance with a Welsh medium. Two years later, he would also be convinced that he embraced the materialized spirit of his mother with the help of two American mediums, William and Eva Thompson. Within days, the Thompsons were exposed as frauds and were arrested at another séance by police officers who found wigs, costumes and fluorescent makeup among their belongings. In spite of this, Doyle was not swayed from his newfound beliefs.

Even before this, a short time after the death of Malcolm Leckie (Doyle's good friend and brother-in-law), a sick friend of Lady Jean Doyle came to stay at the Conan Doyle home. Her name was Lily Lauder-Symonds and she had a reputation for being a gifted medium. While she was there, she conducted a séance for the family and delivered a message from Lady Jean's brother, Malcolm. Years before, the two men had shared a private joke about a guinea that Leckie had had given to Sir Arthur as his first "fee" when he became an Army doctor. Doyle had cherished the small token and wore it on his watch chain. The message that Conan Doyle was given by Lauder-Symonds concerned the guinea, an item that most people, including the medium, knew nothing about. This was likely the incident that finally convinced Sir Arthur of the legitimacy of Spiritualism. Shortly after, he began his full-fledged conversion to the movement, although he did not go public with his beliefs right away due to his involvement with British war efforts.

One of the many spirit photographs that Sir Arthur posed for. In this one, a spirit "extra" is allegedly that of his son, Kingsley, who was killed in the war.

Soon after the war's end, he announced his conversion to the public in the Spiritualist magazine, *The Light*. While Spiritualists around the world applauded his efforts, his critics were instantly unkind. None of them could understand how the creator of the logical detective, Sherlock Holmes, could so gullible about the so-called "wonders" of Spiritualism. But Conan Doyle's convictions came from his supreme self-confidence, and whether the public shared his beliefs of not, he never doubted that he had found the true path. Conan Doyle plunged into Spiritualism with all of the vigor that he showed to everything else, which could be considerable. Despite some setbacks and the exposure of frauds like the Thompsons, Doyle could not be shaken from his beliefs. He was firmly convinced of life after death and the possibility of making contact with the spirit world.

Doyle began lecturing for the Spiritualist cause in October 1917, appearing in Bradford and London. In the years that followed, he visited almost every town in Britain, finding what he described as critical but attentive audiences. It's possible (and perhaps even likely) that most people came primarily to hear the creator of Sherlock

Holmes, but if this was the case, he didn't care. After storming through London, Doyle and his family also visited Australia and the United States, all on behalf of Spiritualism. He also lectured throughout Europe and in South Africa, Kenya and Rhodesia. In 1926, he published a spiritual adventure story called "The Land of the Mist," which featured the popular Professor Challenger character from his earlier book, *The Lost World*. He also wrote a massive, two-volume book called *The History of Spiritualism* and throughout the 1920s, spent a quarter of a million pounds advancing the Spiritualist cause.

During this same time period, Lady Jean began to develop the skills of a medium, which was in sharp contrast to her earlier feelings about the movement. She had disapproved of her husband's interest in the occult and disliked his concerns with Spiritualism, which she called "uncanny and dangerous." However, her brother Malcolm's death during the war changed her feelings and in 1921, she was suddenly given what her husband called the "gift of inspired writing." She soon began to receive messages from the other side and the loved ones they had lost soon began to make regular appearances at the Doyle's home circle.

In his books, writings and personal appearances, Doyle recounted dozens of bizarre and seemingly unexplained occurrences, but whether they were the product of the supernatural or his own willingness to believe is unknown. He often claimed to touch phantom hands, to see objects move about by themselves, to witness the wondrous works of talented mediums and to possess notebooks filled with information that had been given to his wife from spirits --- information that Doyle believed was "utterly beyond her ken." He also came face to face with at least one ghost and investigated a haunted house in Dorset. He chronicled this adventure in his book "On the Edge of the Unknown," which makes compelling reading whether you believe in the mysteries of Spiritualism or not. Strangely, the house burned down after Doyle's investigation and a child's body was found buried in the garden. After the body was found, the haunting ceased and Doyle came to believe that the child's spirit may have been responsible since nothing out of the ordinary ever occurred at the site after the blaze.

Conan Doyle also collected a huge number of spirit photographs, most of which he believed to be genuine, including one of a ghostly woman that was taken at a haunted inn in Norwich. In 1922, he penned a book on the subject called "The Case for Spirit Photography." Unfortunately, the vast majority of the photos that Conan Doyle championed appear blatantly fake today, the obvious results of fraud and double exposure. He became particularly involved with a group of spirit photographers led by William Hope of Crewe. The so-called "Crewe Circle" produced several hundred alleged spirit photographs during its heyday and Doyle posed for a number of them. Not surprisingly, all of the developed plates portrayed a spirit "extra" or two lurking over his shoulder. The credulous author believed all of them to be authentic.

Conan Doyle and Houdini first met in 1920, during the magician's tour of England. The two of them became good friends, despite their opposing views on the supernatural. Houdini was delighted to learn that there was at least one intelligent person who believed in Spiritualism and found that man in his friend Conan Doyle. The author was convinced of the value of the movement to the world and had given up most of his lucrative writing career to lecture about Spiritualism around the world. He also found that Houdini's knowledge of the spirit world was as

Houdini: Among the Spirits - Page 76

vast as his own, although their attitudes differed.

Doyle agreed with some of Houdini's methods in exposing fraudulent mediums because he believed that their existence damaged the legitimacy of the movement. Lacking his new friend's magical training though, he was less able to see how fraud was accomplished. Houdini worked to try and show the secrets practiced by the fraudulent mediums to Doyle but the author merely insisted that the mediums he knew were good and honest people who would never trick or cheat their followers. Besides that, Doyle stated, just because the feats of the spirits could be duplicated did not mean that they were not real. Just because Houdini could prove that fraud was possible was not enough to convince Doyle that it actually occurred.

The two men's arguments were long and inconclusive, but good-natured. Neither convinced the other to his respective point of view but both of them found their own interest stirred by their meeting and the lengthy correspondences that followed.

It would be a series of strange events over the next two years that would bring this unusual friendship to an end. The rift between them started when Doyle began to publicly take the side of Spiritualists who believed that Houdini accomplished some of his greatest magic using supernatural powers. Houdini had long been working to expose fraudulent mediums in private, in print and during his stage shows, which made him a much-hated figure in Spiritualist circles. Some believed they had an explanation for this: Houdini's exposure of mediums was simply to cover the fact that he was a medium himself! They claimed that many of his extraordinary escapes were actually done by Houdini "dematerializing" from the traps that he had placed himself in. "This ability", Doyle stated publicly, "to unbolt locked doors is undoubtedly due to Houdini's mediumistic powers and not to any normal operation of the lock. The effort necessary to shoot a bolt from within a lock is drawn from Houdini the medium, but it must not be thought that this is the only means by which he can escape from his prison. For at times, his body can be... dematerialized and withdrawn."

Now, Houdini was placed in the classic magician's "catch" position, meaning that he could only go so far in denying the Spiritualist claims. By revealing any more, he would have to expose how his escapes were accomplished, which he could never do, not if he wanted to keep drawing audiences. His reply was simply that all of his escapes were managed by purely physical means. He stated that his crusade against Spiritualism was simply a way to protect the general public from charlatans while he kept an open mind on the subject and did not assume that all mediums were frauds.

But this would not be enough to save their friendship, which would soon come to a crashing end.

THE MAN FROM BEYOND

After returning to America from Britain, Houdini launched another movie venture -- after first turning down offers from both the Keith and the Orpheum entertainment companies for tours during the fall and winter of 1920. Harry had decided to retire from vaudeville and produce his own films. He formed the Houdini Picture Corporation, with himself as president.

Harry took just ten days to write a script for his first production. The star of the film, Houdini, would be chopped from a block of ice, where he had been frozen one hundred years before, defrosted and forced to cope with the complexities of twentieth-century life.

Much of the footage for *The Man from Beyond* was shot in Fort Lee, New Jersey. The arctic scenes were filmed in Lake Placid, New York, and in May 1921, the company traveled to Niagara Falls for a big rescue sequence. Burton King, who had directed Houdini's serial, *The Master Mystery*, artfully blended shots of the thundering falls with Houdini's dramatic rescue of the film's heroine just before her boat plunged over the edge. It was later said that dummies were used for some shots and that the forty-eight-year-old escape artist had a safety line tied around his waist, but no trickery like this can be seen in the finished film. The reels for *The Man from Beyond* were processed at Houdini's film developing plant and he edited the movie himself, supervising the cuts and splices.

The developing company taxed Harry's bank account for three years. The estimates for work on the new film turned out to be far too low and to raise money to cover the costs, he took the film on tour, taking advantage of the box-office battles between the Keith and Shubert theater companies. He ended up signing on with the Keith chain for a huge sum and he showed the film along with performing escape stunts and illusions.

The world premiere of *The Man from Beyond* was held in April at the Times Square Theater. The film had its flaws but critics agreed that the Niagara Falls scene alone was worth the price of admission. "It has a whale of a punch," Variety said. "Houdini does a sensational rescue of the heroine in the Niagara rapids on the verge of the cataract and I almost cheered when they made the crawl to safety." A writer for the *Tribune* stated, "There is no fake about this; Houdini actually does it."

Harry, always the showman, was taking no chances with the opening of his first movie production, which explored themes of reincarnation and suspended animation. His personal appearances at the Times Square Theater featured the Vanishing Elephant, which had not been seen since the long run at the Hippodrome. He borrowed an elephant for the feat from the Ringling Brothers Circus. When the pachyderm entered the wooden cabinet, the rear curtains of the stage were raised. When the elephant disappeared, the audience saw the bare brick wall through the box. Once again, the stunt was impossible to explain.

The combined Houdini live and film show ran for three weeks, giving Harry every reason to believe that his future as a movie producer, director and star was ensured.

HOUDINI PICTURE CORPORATION

presents

HOUDINI

in

"THE MAN FROM BEYOND"

Houdini in the river during a scene from *The Man from Beyond*

THE FRIENDSHIP ENDS

Doyle's connections to the Spiritualists who badgered Houdini did much to strain the friendship between the two men. The situation was damaged even more by an event that occurred during Conan Doyle's American lecture tour in May 1922. Things got off to a rocky start when Doyle landed in New York and gave a press conference that was derided and harshly criticized in the *New York Times* the following day. He didn't let this bother him; he was delighted with his tour manager, Lee Keedick, and managed to catch up with a number of old friends. His first lecture, at Carnegie Hall, took place during a heat wave and the humidity inside of the packed lecture room was intense. A record-breaking crowd filled the building and they listened attentively as he spoke for more than an hour about the mysteries of the next world. The following day, a much kinder article appeared in the *New York World*:

Sir Arthur Conan Doyle made an extraordinary impression last night at Carnegie Hall, in his attempt to prove the existence of life after death and the possibility of communication with the dead. The effectiveness of his talk depended on the fact that in spite of the imagination of his writings, he seems to be a downright person. He does not look a man who could be easily stampeded. His audience was profoundly attentive. Evidently, it was a crowd which had its dead.

Doyle gave seven lectures in New York, all of which were well received. He was later to tell Houdini that his lecture tour had raised $125,000, all of which was earmarked for the Spiritualist cause. He spoke of his own experiences with mediums and at séances and showed lantern slides of spirit photographs, mediums exuding ectoplasm and more. Some of the events at the lectures were on the unsettling side, though. Women fainted when the strange, spectral faces glowed on the screen, accompanied by eerie strains of music from a Victrola. Others called out, begging for word from their dead loved ones. Every new slide brought a chorus of screams, moans and fainting spells. Distracted people wandered up and down the aisles, some sobbing uncontrollably. When each lecture ended, Doyle's dressing room was packed with well wishers.

It was a weird and chilling series of talks, and things were going to get worse. Newspaper reports of Doyle's New York lectures caused an extraordinary rush of suicides by people who wanted to see the "next world" immediately. Several of them made front page news. One woman, Maude Fancher, heard Doyle giving a speech on the radio and then murdered her infant son and consumed the contents of a bottle of Lysol cleaner. Before she swallowed the poison, which took a week to kill her, she wrote a letter to Conan Doyle and told him that Spiritualism inspired her to the act. Then, she left a detailed letter for her husband explaining that she wanted her baby nestled in her arms when she was placed in the tomb.

Massive crowds turned out to hear Conan Doyle during his 1922 lecture tour in America

A Brooklyn potter, Frank Alexi, stabbed his wife in the head with an ice pick, claiming that he had seen an evil spirit sitting there that had followed him home from Carnegie Hall. A young man killed himself and his roommate because, he explained, "there were no gas bills in the afterlife."

Conan Doyle, when confronted with these and several other peculiar incidents, stated without hesitation that they were the result of "a misunderstanding of what Spiritualism is meant to be."

This bit of bad press must have encouraged Doyle to get away from the thick of things and meet with a number of mediums with whom he was familiar. He attended séances, including one in which a "spirit" continually referred to him as "Sir Sherlock Holmes." At another, an apparition appeared from a spirit cabinet with the face of Doyle's late mother. When he grasped the spirit to embrace her, he was stunned to find the muscular shoulders of a man beneath the "spirit robes." Rather than expose the medium on the spot, Doyle waited to do it privately. Before he could so, the medium was caught in a hoax. When Doyle was accused of aiding in the fraud, he related the story of the séance --- but no one would believe him and he was savaged in the newspapers.

With this added pressure, a meeting with his friend Houdini must have seemed a welcome respite. The two dined together and then returned to the magician's New York apartment. There, he tried to explain to Doyle how the glove-like paraffin casts, supposedly of spirit hands, were created. A rubber glove would be filled with air, the wrist packed with wood, and then it would be dipped in paraffin wax. If fingerprints were needed, the first step would be to get a mold of a hand in dental wax or plaster; an impression would be made of the palm side of the hand, then of the back, and the two sides would be fitted together. Next, the entire hand would be duplicated in rubber and the fingerprints preserved. Once it was dipped in the paraffin, the process was complete. Doyle refused to accept this as the only explanation for the otherworldly hands that appeared at séances -- maintaining that just because it could be duplicated by ordinary means did not mean that it was not created by supernatural means in the first place.

On June 2, Doyle appeared as the guest of honor invited by Houdini at a banquet given by the Society of American Magicians at the Hotel McAlpin on Broadway. He solemnly announced to the assembled group that he would show something that was "psychic" and "preternatural" only in the sense that it as "not nature as we can now observe it." After building up an atmosphere of excitement and expectation, Doyle ordered the lights to be put out. Suddenly, the audience was astonished to see an actual film of prehistoric creatures, including an iguanodon, a tyrannosaur and a brontosaurus, clawing and biting in a primeval swamp. A smug Doyle told the audience that the motion picture would speak for itself and he would answer no questions about it. The following day, the New York Times ran a breathless story that was headlined "Dinosaurs Cavort on Film for Doyle." They pondered whether "these pictures were intended by the famous author as a joke on the magicians or a genuine pictures... was not revealed."

The next day, Doyle sent a humor-filled letter to Houdini, which he released to the press. He revealed that the films had come from sequences in a motion picture version of his book, *The Lost World*, which was being produced in Chicago. Willis O'Brien, who would later go one to make the acclaimed original version of King Kong, had done the animation of the creatures.

Needing a break from his hectic, and sometimes controversial, schedule in New York, the Conan Doyles went to Atlantic City. Sir Arthur sent a message to Houdini and suggested that he join them at the Hotel Ambassador for a short vacation. Houdini enthusiastically accepted and soon, Doyle was floating in the hotel swimming pool and admiring the length of time that the magician could remain under water, holding his breath. Houdini taught the Doyles' two sons how to dive and float. The children, already dedicated Spiritualists, told the magician that they had no fear of death because they were certain their souls would survive. While Lady Jean and the children played with a beach ball, Doyle and Houdini sat in deck chairs, looking out over the ocean and discussing aspects of Spiritualism. As Conan Doyle described the work done by a London spirit photographer named Ada Deane, Houdini maintained a stoic silence, knowing that Mrs. Deane had been caught substituting a photographic plate from her purse for one exposed at a séance. As the discussion went on Houdini offered comments and careful observations but he had no intention of upsetting his friend and ruining their peaceful and enjoyable holiday.

A photo of Houdini and the Doyles in Atlantic City in 1922, just before the ill-fated seance with Lady Jean

On Sunday, Bess Houdini joined the happy group. Sir Arthur was pleased to see her, as was Harry, who had been enjoying the time spent playing with the Doyle children. He had been entertaining them with small magic tricks and delighted in their laughter. He and Bess were sitting on the beach one afternoon when a young lifeguard's son came running to tell them that Lady Jean wanted to give Houdini a private séance in her suite. Houdini, who was impressed with Lady Jean's obvious sincerity and decency, was thrilled. Perhaps he could at last obtain proof of survival after death! When Conan Doyle later told him that Lady Jean would try and get a message to the magician from his mother, he was beside himself.

Harry went up to the suite with Doyle and Lady Jean greeted him there with great affection. She sat down at a large table, where a pile of paper and a pencil lay ready. Doyle sat next to his wife and Houdini sat on the opposite side of the table. Conan Doyle then offered a solemn prayer and asked his wife if she was ready. Her hand struck the table three times (a Spiritualistic code for "yes") and then she sank into a deep trance.

Houdini wrote later: "I had made up my mind that I would be as religious as it was in my power to be and not at any time did I scoff during the ceremony. I excluded all earthly thoughts and gave my whole soul to the séance. I was willing to believe, even wanted to believe. It was weird to me and with a beating heart I waited, hoping that I might feel once more the presence of my beloved mother..."

Jean began to breathe deeply and her eyes fluttered. Her hand, as though moving on its own, dashed with amazing speed across sheets of paper. Conan Doyle handed them one by one over to the magician. Houdini turned pale and began to tremble. The message began: "Oh my darling, thank God, thank God, at last I'm through. I've tried, oh so often -- now I am happy. Why, of course, I want to talk to my boy -- my own beloved boy -- friends, thank you, with all my heart for this." The message continued with an expression of joy about Mrs. Weiss' new life and the beauty of the next world. She concluded with "I wanted, oh so much -- now I can rest in peace." Doyle then asked Houdini if he wanted to ask his mother a question for "her reply will prove that she is at your side."

Houdini looked extremely upset and could not speak. Conan Doyle suggested a question. "Can my mother read my mind?" Houdini silently nodded his agreement and Lady Jean's hand began to move again. "I always wanted to read my beloved son's mind," the message continued, "there is so much that I want to say to him." The message then went on for several hundred words, mostly expressing joy at communicating with her son and her appreciation of the Doyles.

At the end of the séance, Houdini sank back in his chair, utterly drained and exhausted. Then, unseen by Doyle and Lady Jean, Houdini scribbled with a fragment of pencil a small note on the first sheet of paper. "Message written by Lady Doyle claiming the spirit of my dear mother had control of her hand --- my sainted mother could not write English and spoke broken English." A moment later, he picked up a sheet of paper and boldly wrote on it a single word: "Powell." He looked at Conan Doyle and his eyes issued a challenge to the older man. He had been thinking of his friend Frederick Eugene Powell, a fellow magician who was about to go on the road with one of Houdini's touring companies to promote the film *The Man From Beyond*. If his mother had been reading his mind, wouldn't she have known this?

But Doyle misunderstood the message completely and he stood up from his chair in shock. A good friend of Doyle's, Ellis Powell, editor of the *London Financial News*, had died just three days earlier. He was convinced that Houdini, with the gift of a medium, was trying to say that Powell was in the room. Houdini didn't have the heart to disillusion them on the spot but a few days later, he sent Doyle a letter to let him know that he was thinking of his magician friend and that he was not trying to tell him that a spectral presence was in the room.

Houdini left the hotel and returned to New York to wrestle with his conscience. Should he disclose the truth, that his mother had not come through, that this had been her birthday and there was no reference made to it, that he felt no presence in the room, no scent of her favorite perfume --- and that when the message ended, he felt as alone and lost as he had when she died? If he were to reveal this, the Doyles would be hurt and perhaps even ruined. On the other hand, if he kept quiet, he would be allowing the Spiritualists a false victory. Out of decency, he decided to withhold any statements about the séance until after the Doyles left America.

The Doyles never expected the blow that awaited them. They remained friendly with Houdini, dining and attending the theater with him and he came to the dock to see them off when their ship departed on June 24. For some reason, Houdini held back on speaking out about the Doyles until December 19, 1922. At that time, he issued a release that stated there was not the slightest evidence that his mother had "come through" Lady Jean. His mother could not read or write and could barely speak English and in addition to that, Lady Jean had started her automatic writing by scrawling a cross on the top of the paper. His mother had been Jewish and would have never have done this.

Conan Doyle protested Houdini's claims, stating that language and earthly dates meant nothing to the spirits but Houdini was not convinced. He did not think that the Doyles had deliberately tried to trick him but had deceived themselves by their own gullibility. As for the Doyles, they weathered Houdini's criticisms, although his statement further damaged their once-friendly relationship. Doyle tried to remain loyal to the magician and convinced himself that Houdini was too nervous about the encounter with his mother's spirit to admit that it was genuine. Sir Arthur and lady Jean also claimed in some reports that another message had also come through that day claiming that Houdini would die soon, and this was the reason he denied the authenticity of the communication.

For a short time after this, the two men tried to pretend that their friendship had not been ruined but it was too late to salvage it for the hurt was too deep on both sides. To the Doyles, Houdini was willfully blind and appallingly ungrateful but to Houdini, the Doyles had made a terrible mockery of the deep feelings that he had for his mother. What little remained of their friendship was destroyed in 1923 with Houdini's attacks on medium Mina Crandon, the wife of a Boston surgeon, who appeared under the stage name of Margery. Houdini had become a member of a panel that was sponsored by *Scientific American* magazine to investigate self-proclaimed mediums and Houdini was instrumental in making sure that Margery was discredited. Doyle, who supported Margery, was outraged. "The commission is, in my opinion, a farce," he wrote, "and has already killed itself."

The entire matter with Houdini, Margery and the *Scientific American* investigations was never settled to anyone's satisfaction. Margery was never deemed genuine by the panel but she remained triumphant in the eyes of many, including Conan Doyle. The friendship between he and Houdini had finally reached its bitter end. "You force me to speak," he wrote to the magician, "and I have no wish to offend you but you cannot have it both ways. You cannot bitterly and offensively, often also unruly, attack a subject and yet expect courtesies from those who honor that subject. It is not reasonable."

Within a few years, in 1926, Bess Houdini would be shattered by her husband's premature death. While sorting through his papers and vast library, she uncovered a number of books on Spiritualism and the supernatural and thought they would make a nice gift for Conan Doyle, whom she still considered one of the best friends that Houdini had in life. She wrote to him and offered the books but Doyle was reluctant to take them, believing that Houdini had harbored bad feelings about him at the time of his death. Bess quickly replied that this was not the case and blamed most of the problems between the two men on the press. Houdini had never given up on the possibility of contacting his mother and told Bess so while on his deathbed. And "if, as you believe, he had psychic powers," she wrote, "I give you my word that he never knew it.... He was deeply hurt whenever any journalistic arguments arose between you and would have been the happiest man in the world had he been able to agree with your views on spiritism. He admired and respected you... two remarkable men with different views --- it is usually the third party that distorts the word or the meaning."

INVESTIGATING THE UNEXPLAINED

The Man from Beyond opened at the Rialto Theater in Washington, D.C., in August 1922. Instead of promoting the film with his usual escape stunts, Harry used his time to launch an all-out attack on psychic fraud. Making personal appearances to promote the film, he projected

Houdini in a disguise that he used to infiltrate Spiritualist seances

slides of famous mediums and denounced the deceptions they performed during their séances. In newspaper columns throughout the country he answered questions about the methods used by false mediums. Though he continued to perform in vaudeville, most of Houdini's offstage hours were spent tracking down and exposing what he called "vultures who preyed on the bereaved." Often he attended séances wearing a false beard, mustache or other disguise, behind which he could observe the happenings without being detected. When he had gathered enough evidence to make an exposure, he would leap up, tear off his disguise and shout something like, "I am Houdini! And you are a fraud!"

His activities received extensive press coverage but he was not doing it for the publicity. More than anything, Houdini wanted to find a genuine medium,a real psychic who would put him in touch with his mother.

In addition to visiting mediums and attending séances, Houdini also began to re-enact Spiritualistic manifestations during his stage shows, showing how so-called "spirit forms" and "ectoplasm" could easily be created by a clever magician. Houdini was not the first magician to do this, but his shows were undoubtedly the most dramatic.

From the earliest days of Spiritualism, there had been a

running battle between mediums and magicians. In 1853, just five years after the Fox Sisters gained fame in rural Hydesville, N.Y., a magician named J.H. Anderson of New York issued the first challenge. He offered a monetary award to "any poverty stricken medium" who could produce raps in the public hall where he gave his regular performances. The Fox Sisters were among those who accepted Anderson's challenge, but the magician backed out and, amid catcalls and hisses from the audience, refused to allow the mediums on the stage.

One of the greatest of the early rivalries between mediums and magicians involved the Davenport brothers. Ira and William Davenport were professional mediums who were the first to popularize the spirit cabinet in their performances. This special cabinet had three doors at the front and a bench running lengthwise inside. The center door had a small diamond-shaped opening covered by a curtain, through which various phenomena would manifest. Before each performance, members of the audience were free to inspect the cabinet, and also to make sure that the Davenports, who sat astride the bench, facing one another, were securely tied and unable to move about. Within seconds after the doors were closed, the brothers were able to produce raps, musical sounds and a variety of other effects. During part of the séance, an audience member was even allowed to sit on the bench between the brothers.

Although the phenomena they produced was typical of the Spiritualist séances of the day, the Davenports were ambiguous about their powers. They never presented themselves as Spiritualists but on the other hand, they insisted the manifestations they created were genuine. While in England, they became the subject of controversy. They held séances every night for more than two months in a hall in London. Various committees studied these demonstrations without finding any evidence of fraud but, nevertheless, they were met with widespread public opposition and even hostility.

Early in 1865, the Davenports toured the English provinces and for the most part, the shows did well, but there were a number of problems encountered in some of the towns. At Liverpool, in February, two members of an inspection committee selected by the audience used a complicated knot to secure the brothers. The Davenports protested that the knots were too tight and cut off their circulation, but a doctor who examined them disagreed. They

The Davenport brothers in their spirit cabinet

John Nevil Maskelyne

refused to sit and asked one of their assistants to cut the ropes. A riot broke out and the Davenports quickly left Liverpool.

Finally, in March 1865, the Davenports played at the Cheltenham Town Hall and encountered John Nevil Maskelyne, one of England's original conjurers, and the only investigator ever believed to have uncovered their manifestations as fraud.

Maskelyne was one of the most popular of the early British stage magicians. The son of a saddle maker, he was born in Cheltenham in December 1839. Intrigued as a boy by an entertainer's "dancing dinner plates," he practiced until he was able to keep several dishes whirling about at the same time on a table top. At nineteen, he began working as a clockmaker's apprentice and constructed his first piece of conjuring equipment: a small chest with a secret panel. He could lock a borrowed ring inside, bind the chest with tape, and then secretly extract the ring as he gave the box to a spectator. The box was so well constructed that it managed to withstand even the most rigorous examinations.

On March 7, 1865, Maskelyne attended the séance given by the Davenport brothers at the Cheltenham Town Hall. Although it was the middle of the afternoon, heavy curtains were fastened over the windows to darken the hall. Lamps were used to illuminate the stage where trestles had been erected to support a three-doored wooden cabinet that was similar in size and shape to a large clothing wardrobe. The doors were standing open when Maskelynes entered the hall. Planks seats were nailed down the middle of the cabinet and a guitar, violin and bow, two hand bells, a tambourine and a trumpet had been placed inside.

A lecturer introduced the Davenport brothers and then called for volunteers. Maskelyne and several other men rushed to the front of the theater to inspect the paraphernalia. The committee members lashed the medium's wrists behind their backs and tied their ankles as they sat facing each other in the cabinet. Then, the lecturer closed the doors and signaled for the lamps to be put out.

Almost immediately, bells rang and flew out onto the floor of the stage. Pale, ghostly hands waved through the apertures in the center of the cabinet. A tambourine jangled, a guitar strummed and a violin played eerie music. Yet, when the lamps were lighted and the doors opened, the brothers sat tightly bound, exactly as they had been when the séance had started.

As mentioned, England was sharply divided over whether the Davenports were genuine mediums or clever tricksters. Purely by chance, Maskelyne discovered that they were frauds. A ray of sunlight from a poorly draped window had flashed briefly on the stage during the performance and from his vantage point on the side of the stage, Maskelyne had been able to see into the cabinet through a crack in the door. He saw Ira Davenport vigorously ringing the bell! He knew that if one brother was able to free himself, then the other one could too.

Maskelyne told several people what he had seen but a clergyman who had been watching from the other side of the stage scoffed at this explanation. Determined to prove his point, Maskelyne persuaded a friend to help him build a cabinet so that they could work together and duplicate what the Davenports were doing.

Once they learned the technique of slipping their hands out of, and back into, tightly knotted ropes, producing "spirit music" was easy for the two men. After three months of practice, Maskelyne appeared at Jessop's Gardens on June 19. Trick by trick --- and they stressed they were tricks --- he and his friend duplicated the entire Davenport séance. Five days later, the Birmingham Gazette offered a long account of the performance and showed that Maskelyne had proven that spirits were not necessary for a "spirited" séance. Of course, by then, the Davenports had moved on to the Continent and were being wined and dined by royalty. Most of their audiences had no idea that their clever act has been exposed as just that: an act.

Maskelyne went on to become one of England's most famous magicians. In later years, he would continue to offer "spirit shows" and duplicate the methods of mediums in his performances.

Another pioneering magician in the field of psychical investigation was William S. Marriott. Unfortunately, little is known about Marriott's early years, how he got started in the magic field and what led him to pursue the truth behind Spiritualist mediums. What we do know is that he was described as a likable man with "a pair of well-waxed mustaches" and that he was a British professional magician who performed under the name of Dr. Wilmar. At some point, in the early 1900s, he became interested in exposing the hoaxes that were being carried out by fraudulent mediums. He actually took up this task before magicians like Houdini, who became quite famous for it.

One of his first, and most valuable, exposures came when he located and publicized a copy of a catalog called "Gambols with Ghosts: Mind Reading, Spiritualistic Effects, Mental and

Magician William S. Marriott poses with some of the Spirit medium props that he purchased from the "Gambols with Ghosts" catalog

Psychical Phenomena and Horoscopy." It was a secret catalog that was being circulated among mediums and was filled with tricks, apparatus and paraphernalia that could be used to dupe the public. The catalog was issued in 1901 by Ralph E. Sylvestre of Chicago and was designed for private circulation among mediums, on the understanding that it would be returned to Sylvestre when tricks had been selected from it.

The catalog had an introduction that read: "Our experience during the past 30 years in supplying mediums and others with the peculiar effects in this line enable us to place before you only those which are practical and of use, nothing that you have to experiment with. We wish you to thoroughly appreciate that, while we do not, for obvious reasons, mention the names of our clients and their work (they being kept in strict confidence, the same as a physician treats his patients), we can furnish you with the explanation and, where necessary, the material for the production of any known public 'tests' or 'phenomena' not mentioned in this, our latest list. You are aware that our effects are being used by nearly all prominent mediums of the entire world."

This notorious catalog included equipment for slate-writing, stuffed ghosts, self-playing guitars, self-rapping tables, materializations, and a "Complete Spiritualistic Séance." Marriott obtained a number of these illusions from the catalog and had himself photographed posing with them.

Marriott had become disenchanted with the deceptions being carried out by dishonest mediums. Many deceptive mediums would do whatever they could to bilk unsuspecting clients and sitters out of money while promising to contact their deceased loved ones. While not every medium was dishonest, there were enough of them to color the entire movement -- and to give Spiritualism a bad name.

In 1909, *Pearson's Magazine* approached Marriott in order to conduct, on the magazine's behalf, a series of investigations of spirit mediums. The results were published in a four-part series. In the first installment, he delved into Spiritualist séances and wrote of several hilarious incidents that occurred. At one séance, the medium entered the spirit cabinet as the lights were being turned out and after a time, the curtain parted and a stately form emerged from the cabinet. The "spirit" was partially luminous and carried a shimmering globe in its hand, which it held near its face to make it more visible. The figure graciously inclined its head, gestured as if to bless the sitters, and then retired back into the cabinet. Marriott described what happened next:

This should have closed the séance. Tonight, an unrehearsed effect was in store for the believers. As the form entered the cabinet, he sat down on what he thought was the settee. It happened to be my knees. I had quickly slipped into the curtained enclosure and was sitting, waiting for him to come back. As my arms went around him, he gave a yell followed by language which· I will not repeat. My friend had the light up in a moment. And there for the faithful was the edifying sight of the medium, clothed in flimsy white draperies, struggling in the arms of myself!

Marriott's reputation as an investigator was widely known and he worked hard to show that

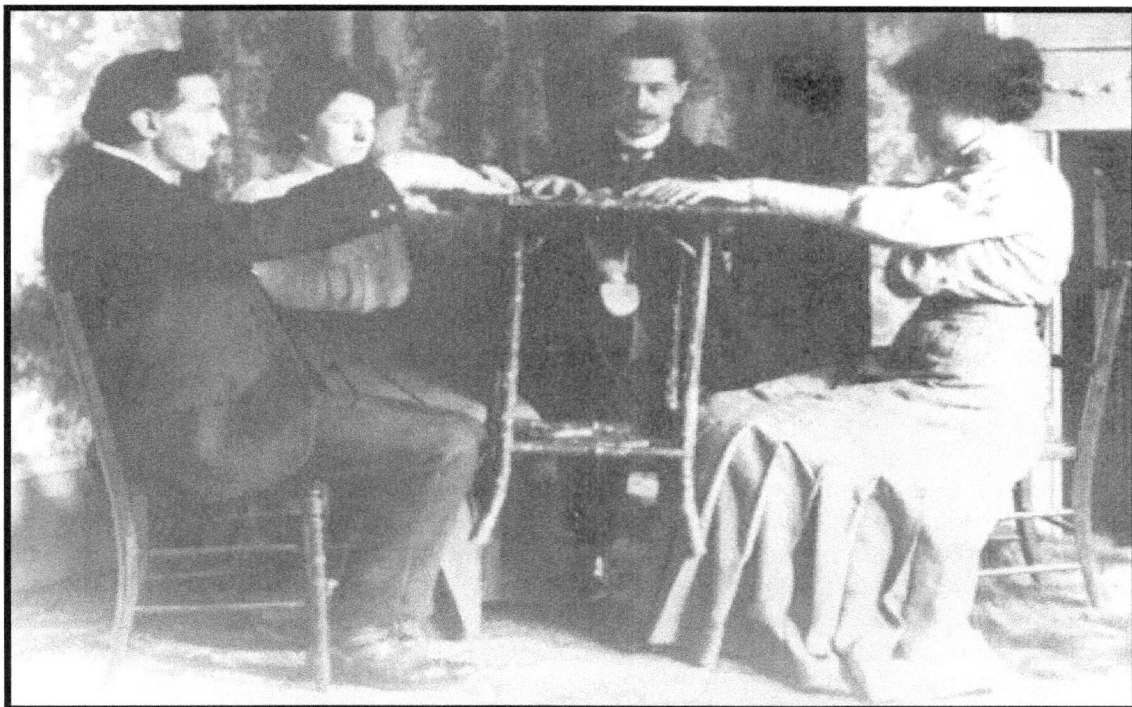

Marriott demonstrated for *Pearson's Magazine* readers how "table tipping" was sometimes accomplished. Notice the well-placed foot under the table!

what some believers thought was impossible could actually be accomplished by a skilled magician. Marriott was so well respected by "both sides of the aisle" because he was not just offering money to anyone who could perform a paranormal feat he could not duplicate. Rather, he was simply showing that alternative explanations to apparent miracles existed and he invited open-minded observes to decide for themselves what they wanted to believe.

"If I am one of the 'scoffers'," wrote Marriott, "it is not because of any original bias, but because of the arrant humbug, cheap trickery, and pathetic self-delusion that I have encountered at every point of my investigations of Spiritualism..."

Magicians like Harry Kellar, Howard Thurston and many others also took to debunking the antics of fraudulent mediums, but none of them did so as successfully as Houdini. But not everything that he witnessed during his psychic investigations could be easily explained away. He kept vast files and records of his investigations and when he died, these reports came into the possession of Joseph Dunninger, a friend of Harry's and a fellow conjurer.

In the wealth of material, there was a record of one case that baffled Houdini. His handwritten account of it was contained in the files, dated in Los Angeles on April 11, 1923. He was approached in reference to photographs that were to be taken of Mrs. Mary Fairfield McVickers who, before she died, requested that photographs be taken of her body at 5:00 p.m. on the afternoon of her funeral. According to reports, she claimed that she would appear in spirit form at that time. Mrs. McVickers made this unusual pronouncement on the occasion of her seventy-third birthday in July 1922. She told her friends at the First Spiritualist Temple of Los Angeles, where she was a member, that she had experienced a vision of her approaching death. "I feel that if a picture is taken over my body about 5:00 p.m. on the day of my funeral, I will appear in spirit form," she told those present at the gathering.

Mrs. McVickers died the following April and one of her friends, Albert H. Hetzel, contacted Houdini and told him about the unusual request the woman had made for a photograph to be taken of her body. Houdini was intrigued and so he got in touch with a friend and movie producer named Larry Semon about borrowing a cameraman.

On the afternoon of the funeral, Nathan B. Moss, who worked for Keystone Press Illustration Service in Hollywood arrived with his camera and plate holders loaded with fourteen negatives. Houdini had not told the man what they would be photographing and he and Moss went to a place called Howland and Dewey, who were Kodak representatives in Los Angeles. Houdini wrote that Moss "had no idea what I wanted but was under the impression that I was going to do a stunt and wanted a stunt picture. I told him that I wanted him to reload his plate holder with brand new plates, which I would buy. He, not knowing the importance of the test, derided the fact of my not wanting to use his plates, but I told him that I might have to take an oath that I bought the plates and that therefore it was important."

When they arrived at the camera store, they asked for a dozen 5X7 plates and the clerk, Frank Hale, pulled out four packages of twelve each. Mat Korn, a customer in the store and a stranger to Houdini, was standing nearby and he was asked to choose one of the packets. He handed it to the magician, but Houdini noticed that one end of the package was not tightly sealed. He asked for five more packages and he asked another customer, identified as a Mr. Wheeler (a photographer for the Los Angeles Record), to choose one for him. Houdini purchased the package of plates and he and Moss entered the darkroom on the premises and removed the plates that Moss had already placed in the camera, substituting them with the brand new plates. He then placed all of the loaded plates into his camera. A few moments later, they left for the church so that they could arrive just before 5:00 p.m.

At the church, the body of Mrs. McVickers had been placed in a white, open casket at the right of the pulpit, surrounded by flowers. Moss then took ten photographs of the scene, each of them taken under the same time exposure of three minutes. In addition to Houdini and Moss, the witnesses included Albert Hetzel, J.M. Hall, Virgil Vlasek and Stanley Bruce of the Los Angeles Examiner.

After the photos were taken, the men left and went immediately to the Keystone Press Illustration office. The plates were developed in Houdini's presence, and on one of them, they noticed a peculiar streak. Houdini wrote: "Mr. Moss made a print from this plate, which caused a great deal of talk. Not one photographer could explain how this could be tricked. Mr. Moss

The mysterious photo from the McVicker's funeral that Houdini was unable to debunk.

offered one hundred dollars to anyone who could produce it under the same conditions, whereas no one could duplicate it." Houdini thought enough of this incident to make a note of it in his personal diary as well. "Took pictures at church," he penned. "A peculiar test."

Dunninger published Houdini's notes in his brochure "Houdini's Spirit Exposees" in 1928 and stated that Houdini offered a number of magicians one thousand dollars if they could duplicate the photo. No one accepted the challenge.

The photograph with the mysterious light was the second one taken. The streak was a heavy band of light that started a few inches from the floor and then extended up to about two feet above a five-foot-high black screen. This screen had been placed between the open casket and the auditorium. At the upper end of the streak, the light became a diffused, glowing mass of a larger shape than the trail that descended from it. Looking closely at the streak, it has an interesting formation, starting as a sharply defined, broad band and then shifting to make two parallel lines. Just before it turns into a glowing mass, a third line starts to appear. A number of photographic experts studied the plate but stated that because of the nature of the image, it would have been practically impossible for it to have been caused by a defective plate, plate holder or camera.

Needless to say, a hoax was out of the question for it would have certainly not helped

Houdini's campaign against fraudulent Spiritualists for him to admit that a "ghost photograph" had been achieved in the church. Even so, he did have the integrity to admit that no satisfactory explanation could be found for the photograph.

Joseph Dunninger wrote that Houdini made no attempt to debunk or explain the photograph. "He did not see the light. It made itself only evident on the photograph," said Dunninger. "This report shows that Houdini was willing to believe if the proof was brought before him... and was willing to give credit whenever credit was due."

Houdini publicly stated: "I am willing to be convinced. My mind is open, but the proof must be such as to leave no vestige of doubt that what is claimed to be done is accomplished only through or by supernatural power."

To prove that he did have an open mind, the magician made a pact with a number of his friends (including Dunninger) that if he should die, he would make contact, if at all possible, from the other side. He devised a secret code with the one person that he trusted most, his wife Bess, so that if a message should arrive from the beyond, she would be able to determine that it was really from Houdini. Some have suggested that Houdini came up with the idea of the "death pact" because he was already receiving some foreboding of his death (which was just three years away) but this is not the case. He merely wanted to demonstrate that he believed in the possibility of the other side.

And while Houdini may have been willing to believe in the unexplainable, he was still unwilling to suffer those he considered to be fools and frauds. In 1923, he took time off from his vaudeville engagements to travel across the country on a lecture crusade against fraudulent mediums. His book, *A Magician Among the Spirits*, would be published the following year. It was a scathing look at the fraud that was being accomplished by fake mediums around the country.

HALDANE OF THE SECRET SERVICE

Houdini continued his fascination with film and now, as a producer, he found himself in a quandary. He faced a choice of three scripts for his next independent film: *Il Mistero di Osiris or The Mystery of the Jewel* -- a story of Ancient Egypt; *Yar, the Primeval Man* -- the adventures of a caveman; and *Mr. Yu or Haldane of the Secret Service*. It was a difficult decision because had had great faith in the screenwriter -- Houdini had written all of the scripts himself. Finally, *Mr. Yu* was chosen but he shortened the name to *Haldane of the Secret Service*.

In the film, Heath Haldane (played by Houdini) fights a gang of counterfeiters that had been chasing Adele Ormsby (played by Gladys Leslie). The gangsters throw the Secret Service man into the Hudson River, and he is rescued by a passing boat. Reviving quickly, Haldane swims out to a passing ocean liner and is taken on board after climbing hand over hand up a rope. Haldane goes on to track down phony bank notes in Hull and London (using footage shot in England), then he visit's the Apache Café in Paris, where he learns the counterfeit bills are being produced in an old French monastery. The "monks" trap him and lash him to a large wheel. With his hands and feet manacled and rushing torrents of water engulfing him, he manages to escape, round up the criminal gang and unmask their "Chinese" leader as the heroine's father. The picture ends with the girl safely in Haldane's arms.

The film received only lukewarm reviews. Houdini was no Valentino. His shy, restrained love scenes hardly made women in American movie houses swoon. The films were sold on sensational value alone. Regrettably, there was nothing in the new film to match the Niagara Falls rescue in The Man from Beyond or the fantastic escapes of the earlier films. Harry read the reviews with dismay and compared his cost sheets with his income statements and found them severely disappointing.

Sadly, he canceled his pending productions and Houdini brought his career as a movie producer to an abrupt halt. He never made another film.

Houdini with the cast and crew of *Haldane of the Secret Service*

Harry was still faced with the task of trying to recoup some of the expenses from his last picture. He mounted an extensive advertising campaign for the film. Giant cutout figures of Houdini, manacled in a diving position, were made available for display in the front of theaters. Thousands of small slips of paper were printed with a message that read, "This lock is not HOUDINI-proof. He could pick it as easily as you pick a daisy. See the Master-Man of Mystery HOUDINI in *'Haldane of the Secret Service'*, a picture that will thrill you to your marrows." The notes were inserted in the keyholes of doors in cities were the movie was shown.

Harry devised a novel stunt for publicizing the film. Two men carrying identical black satchels met on a busy downtown street. One man shouted that the other had taken his bag. After their dispute drew a crowd, one of the satchels was opened, and the two men whipped out a large cloth banner and held it up for all to see. The banner was printed with the name of the film and the theater where it was showing.

Houdini also spread rumors like the ones that had helped draw attention to *The Grim Game*. Reporters were told that the giant waterwheel had broken as it whirled him around. He claimed that he had almost drowned before he could free himself from the wreckage. It garnered some publicity but it wasn't enough. Haldane of the Secret Service was a financial disaster -- although it did have its compensations. The films raised Houdini's stature as a public figure even higher than it had been before and managed to raise his theater and vaudeville salaries to the highest in his career.

..AND THEY NEVER SPOKE AGAIN

In 1923, Houdini joined a committee that was put together by *Scientific American* magazine, which offered a reward for any medium able to prove that their psychical gifts were genuine. The initial prize for an authentic exhibition was $2,500. There was also a secondary prize for anyone who could produce a genuine spirit photograph. The committee consisted of Dr. William McDougall, professor of psychology at Harvard; Dr. Daniel Fisk Comstock, from the Massachusetts Institute of Technology; Dr. Walter Franklin Prince, research officer for the American Society for Psychical Research; Hereward Carrington, prolific writer on the occult; and Houdini.

The committee had been Houdini's idea. He had been approached by the magazine to write a series of articles on Spiritualism but, because of his vaudeville commitments, could not accept the offer. He suggested instead the formation of an investigative committee on which he would serve for no fee -- if he were granted the right to select or reject its other members. Harry did not exercise his power of approval to limit committee membership to people he knew would agree with him. The committee would eventually have several members with whom Houdini could not get along. Even the original membership was problematic. Houdini's personal opinion of Carrington, for example, was that the writer was an opportunist who professed to believe in Spiritualism because it was a good way to sell his books about the occult.

Before Houdini left on a cross-country vaudeville tour, he promised to cancel his bookings whenever he was called for an investigation. The Water Torture Cell was still the main feature of his act and the open air straitjacket escape continued to tie up traffic in the cities and to draw capacity crowds for his performances.

It was in Denver that Houdini crossed paths with his estranged friend, Sir Arthur Conan Doyle. During Doyle's first lecture tour of America, Houdini, with difficulty, had avoided a public controversy with his friend. Now, as newspaper headlines spoke of Sir Arthur's "spirit truths," counter-arguments from Houdini began making the wire services. In Denver, the Doyles and their children were Houdini's guests at the Orpheum Theater. Harry sent a box of candy to their young daughter and a bouquet of violets for Lady Doyle. In his dressing room after the show, Harry and Sir Arthur were again at odds over whether or not spirit photographs could be produced by trickery. The next day, Doyle, when they met, insisted that a couple called Julius and Agnes Zancig were genuine mediums. Harry knew otherwise. In 1906, the Zancigs had been with him on the road. Julius Zancig was a member of the Society of American Magicians and Houdini once bought an act from him, complete with all of the silent and spoken cues. He added it to the collection and sometimes pulled it out when he wanted a convincing "mind-reading" act. While the Zancigs had an impressive mind-reading act and were billed as "Two Minds With but a Single Thought," were no more psychics, Houdini stated, than he was.

On May 9, 1923, the *Denver Express* newspaper ran the following story:

DOYLE IN DENVER DEFIES HOUDINI AND OFFERS TO BRING DEAD BACK AGAIN

Sir Arthur Conan Doyle, here to preach the gospel of spiritism, is going to back his psychic forces with $5,000 against the skepticism of Harry Houdini, the magician, who recently asserted that all séance manifestations were fakes. The famous writer so asserted on his arrival from Colorado Springs late yesterday when informed Houdini was also in Denver.

"Houdini and I have discussed spiritism before," said Sir Arthur. "I have invited him to attend a sitting with me, each of us backing our beliefs with $5,000. I have even offered to bring my dead mother before him in physical form and to talk to her. But we have never got together on it."

The Doyles met the Houdinis that evening in the lobby of the Brown Palace Hotel. Sir Arthur was apologetic, explaining to Harry that the newspaper had put words in his mouth. Houdini was very understanding. He had not seen the article, but he knew that reporters sometimes misquoted people. He was sorry to have to miss Doyle's lecture at the Ogden Theater because of his own performance at the theater that night, but Bess was going to accept the Doyles' invitation to attend and she would tell Harry all about it later.

On Doyle's recommendation, Houdini and his assistant, Jim Collins, went to see Alexander Martin, a Denver photographer whose pictures of the living also showed "spirit extras," or the faces of the dead. Martin posed Harry in a straight-backed chair with Collins standing behind him. When the plate was developed, the print showed four ghostly faces in the background: two bearded men, an Indian and a shrouded woman. The next day, Harry returned for another sitting and this time, he posed alone. Five "spirit extras" appeared on the print: four bearded men and one who wore a mustache. Three of the "spirits" wore glasses. Houdini almost burst out laughing when he saw that the man with the mustache was the late Theodore Roosevelt.

Harry may have been amused, but he was not impressed. He believed that Martin was using a simple double-exposure technique. Before his arrival, he surmised that Martin had snipped the heads from other photographs, put them on a black background, and exposed the plate, masking the area in the center. With this prepared plate, ghostly extras would "materialize" when Martin photographed his subject. Houdini later created his own spirit photographs in New York. In one of them, he clasped his own spirit self in his arms and in another, Abraham Lincoln

To prove the ease in which fraudulent spirit photographs could be created, Houdini experimented with many of his own at his home in New York.

At left, Houdini causes "ectoplasm" to appear from his mouth and take the shape of a woman's features.

And below, Houdini appears with the ghost of Abraham Lincoln, a photo which was inspired by an allegedly genuine photo in which the "ghost" of Theodore Roosevelt materialized with him as a spirit "extra".

appeared with him.

Meanwhile, there had been no rush of applicants for the *Scientific American* prizes. It was easy for a photographer to produce mysterious photos on his own plates, in his own studio, or for a medium to conjure up phenomena when surrounded by hymn-singing believers. Why would they risk their reputations being tested by observers who were well versed in psychology, physics and trickery?

A few mediums did come forward. The first to announce that she was ready to try for the prize was Elizabeth Allen Thomson, but she was never formally tested, having been caught with twenty yards of gauze taped to her groin, flowers tucked under her breasts

and a live snake concealed in her armpit. A contestant who looked more promising was George Valiantine. He had given two séances for *Scientific American* while Houdini was on the road. The first had been unimpressive. During the second, a trumpet had floated in the dark, lifted by a spirit Indian, according to the medium, at least. The trumpet tapped various sitters, whacked a spectator's head, and then crashed to the floor just as Fred Keating, a young magician friend of Hereward Carrington, tried to grab it.

Houdini attended the third séance and this time, science was brought into the séance room. Unknown to the medium, men in an adjoining chamber were following his movements with light signals, a Dictaphone and a stopwatch. Valiantine's chair had been wired. Whenever he left his seat, a light flashed in the control room and a note was made of the time. By comparing the times that Valiantine got out of his chair and the times when phenomena was recorded in the séance room, it was obvious that it was the medium, not the spirits, who had been raising a ruckus in the dark. The *New York Times* quoted Houdini when the medium was exposed.

J. Malcolm Bird, an associate editor of the magazine and the secretary for the investigative committee, was annoyed by the newspaper story. The *Times* reporter should not have written the story until he, Bird, had printed an article in *Scientific American*. He resented being scooped. When the *Times* followed up with an interview with Houdini, Bird was enraged. The medium-trapping system had been devised before Houdini, who was busy with his vaudeville tour, came on the scene. Yet to the public, it appeared that the magician had exposed Valiantine. Bird disliked Houdini immensely. This would be the first time the two men clashed, but it would not be the last.

In California, Conan Doyle was upset by another newspaper story. Quotes from Houdini in the *Oakland Tribune* were "full of errors." He had to "utterly contradict" them. Perhaps Sir Arthur had forgotten he had been misquoted in Denver. Harry replied that he had given the Oakland reporter material for a single article, which had been expanded into a series. He couldn't help the fact that his statements had been misconstrued. By this time, the friendship between the two men had reached a point that it was almost beyond repair.

Houdini spent more time attacking fraudulent mediums than arranging spectacular escapes during his fall vaudeville tour. In late September, he spoke to a psychology class at the University of Illinois on "The Psychology of Audiences" and "The Negative Side of Spiritualism." The latter topic took up most of the class time. In October, he gave an illustrated lecture on mediums and their methods at Marquette University.

Meanwhile, medium Nino Pecoraro applied for the *Scientific American* prize money while Houdini was still on the road with his lecture tour. Conan Doyle, during his first American lecture tour, had attended a séance held by Pecoraro and had been tremendously impressed by him. He noted that the medium, while bound with wire, caused a bell to ring, a tambourine to spin in the air, and a toy piano to play. Hereward Carrington, a committee member, had actually arranged the séance for Doyle. There was reason to think that the committee might give Pecoraro a comparatively sympathetic hearing.

Doubtlessly believing that Pecoraro would have too easy a time of it, *Scientific American* publisher Orson Munn urgently requested Houdini, then playing in Little Rock, Arkansas, to return to New York and attend a test séance. Fellow committeemen planned to tie the Italian medium with a sixty-foot-long rope and Houdini laughed. Even amateur escapologists could free their hands when trussed up in such a manner, he told them. Houdini slashed the rope into short lengths and secured the medium himself. After that, the medium produced no manifestations.

Houdini returned to his theater tour in the Midwest. He spoke at several more colleges, which became rehearsals for a lecture tour that was booked for him around the country. His anti-Spiritualism campaign had been only for his spare time during his Orpheum tour. Now he was free -- at least for twenty one-night shows -- to devote his full energy to counteracting the propaganda that was being spread by people like Sir Arthur Conan Doyle.

Houdini's lectures were a huge success. The people who attended the shows came more to see him perform than to hear about his exposures of the Spiritualists. He found that he had to mix entertainment with his message to appeal to the crowds. To say that a medium employed a trick spirit slate was not enough. He had to show how the slate was used. The actual

Nino Pecoraro, one of the applicant's for the *Scientific American* award, and Houdini. The medium showed great promise in the seance room until Houdini tied him up. After that, his "mysterious" powers vanished.

demonstration drove his point home and delighted the audiences at the same time. To make sure that he had full auditoriums to educate, he broke out of challenge packing boxes at every stop along his route to generate publicity.

The publication of Houdini's book *A Magician Among the Spirits* in 1924 brought violent attacks from believers, cheers from the skeptics and the inevitable end of his friendship with Sir Arthur. Houdini wrote that he treasured Doyle as a friend. Sir Arthur was a "brilliant man," he had a "great mind" -- except where Spiritualism was concerned. Houdini respected Doyle's beliefs and was convinced that he was sincere, but the eminent author refused to accept the fact that many of the mediums he endorsed were frauds. Houdini listed instance after instance of mediums that Sir Arthur trusted even though others had found them to be frauds. He quoted the written message that Lady Doyle claimed had come from his mother in Atlantic City --- then revealed why it could not have been from her spirit.

Doyle was angered and saddened by the book. He had been fascinated with Houdini the man, but when his friend attempted to destroy his beliefs and held him up to ridicule, any further friendship between them was impossible.

Houdini and Conan Doyle never wrote or spoke to one another again.

THE 'MARGERY' AFFAIR

Houdini returned to his lecture circuit after the Pecoraro fiasco, only to hear three months later that the investigative panel had deadlocked over a medium named Mina Crandon, who used the stage name of "Margery". They stated that they believed her to be genuine and were prepared to give her the $2,500 reward. J. Malcolm Bird was one of Crandon's supporters and was eager to give her the magazine's endorsement. He allowed word of the panel's favorable findings to reach the press. "Boston Medium Baffles Experts," one headline announced. "Houdini the Magician Stumped," trumpeted another.

Houdini, who had not even been present during Crandon's séances, much less stumped by them, was stunned to think the magazine would even consider approving a medium that he had never seen. Publisher Orson Munn called him in for a consultation and he publicly told *Scientific American* that he would forfeit $1,000 of his own money if he failed to expose Margery as a fraud.

When it was discovered that Houdini was now going to be involved in the investigations of Margery, Sir Arthur Conan Doyle, an avid supporter of the medium, was outraged. He called it a "capital error" placing such an enemy of Spiritualism into the investigation. He wrote: "The Commission is, in my opinion, a farce." Mina Crandon, however, seemed to welcome the opportunity to test her mettle against Houdini. The prize money meant nothing to this wealthy woman but the opportunity to win the approval of such a prestigious committee --- at the expense of the mighty Houdini --- proved too great a temptation for her to resist.

Houdini traveled with Orson Munn by train to Boston and on the way, he reviewed the findings of his colleagues on the investigative panel. To his way of thinking, the investigation had been badly handled from the start. Margery did not perform under the same test conditions that other mediums were forced to. She was allowed to hold her test séances at her home in Boston, which opened things up widely for the possibility of fraud. Most of the committee members had availed themselves of the Crandons' generous hospitality during the proceedings, staying in their home, eating their food and enjoying their company. Houdini believed that this had badly compromised their objectivity and later, it was learned that accepting food and a bed from the Crandons were the least of the problems. One investigator had actually borrowed money from Margery's husband, while another hoped to win his backing for a research foundation. Worse yet, the "distinguished" panel was not unaware of Margery's physical attractions. Years later, at least one committee member would tell of his amorous encounters with the shapely medium.

Mina Crandon certainly created a firestorm of controversy in the early 1920s. In truth, she was a rather unlikely medium.

Mina Stinson had been born in Ontario in 1888, the daughter of a farmer. She moved to Boston when she was sixteen so that she could play the piano, coronet and cello in local bands and orchestras. After working as a secretary, an actress and an ambulance driver, she married a grocer named Earl P. Rand, with whom she had a son. They remained happily married until a medical operation introduced her to Le Roi Goddard Crandon, a prominent surgeon and a former instructor at the Harvard Medical School. She divorced Rand in 1918 and married Crandon a short time later.

Mina had no psychic experiences early in her life and in fact, had no interest in the spirit world at all until her husband became enthralled with the paranormal in the early 1920s. One evening in May 1923, Dr. Crandon invited a number of friends to his home for a "home circle" meeting. The group gathered around a small table and soon had it tilting in response to the sitters' questions. Crandon suggested that they each remove their hands from the table, one at a time, to see which individual was responsible for the paranormal activity. One by one, each of them took their hands away but the

The young and lovely medium Mina Crandon, who used the pseudonym of "Margery". She would become Houdini's greatest nemesis in his battle against fraudulent mediums. The "Margery Affair" would always have many questioning just how far Houdini would go to expose a medium.

table only stopped rocking when the last of the sitters lifted her hands. Dr. Crandon had solved the mystery: the medium was his own wife.

At first, the idea of being a medium seemed like a lark to the fun-loving Mina. Throughout the summer of 1923, the Crandons held one séance after another at their home. Each time, Mina seemed to exhibit some new ability. It seemed that Dr. Crandon only had to read about some new spirit manifestation before his wife could duplicate it.

Within a month of her first official séance, Dr. Crandon announced a plan to place his wife under hypnosis so that they could try and make contact with the psychic control who would serve as her spirit guide. At first, Mina resisted this idea, claiming that she didn't want to miss any of the "fun" while she was under hypnosis. Eventually, however, she gave in to her husband's wishes and soon, a deep male voice made itself heard to the Crandon home circle.

The voice turned out to belong to Mina's brother, Walter Stinson, who had been crushed to death in a railroad accident in 1911. From this point on, Walter's spirit was a regular presence in the Crandon séance room. He proved to have a strong personality, a quick wit and was given to using salty language. Many visitors to the séance room became convinced of what they heard simply because they could not imagine that such coarse and vulgar language would come from the mouth of the pretty doctor's wife. A number of observers noted that Walter's voice did not seem to come from Mina at all. The sound seemed to emanate from another part of the room and would continue even when Mina was in a trance or had her mouth filled with water. The effect seemed so remarkable that one skeptic, searching for a plausible explanation for what he had experienced, wondered if perhaps Mina was able to speak through her ears! Walter became well known as Mina's spirit guide and, along with his sister, began to find fame all over the world.

But Mina hardly needed Walter's help to become a popular medium, especially among her male sitters. Mina resembled nothing so much as a light-hearted flapper. Even Houdini conceded that she was an exceedingly attractive woman, and one psychic researcher warned his colleagues to "avoid falling in love with the medium." She usually greeted her sitters wearing a flimsy dressing gown, bedroom slippers and silk stockings. This attire, leaving almost nothing to the imagination, was supposedly intended to rule out the possibility of trickery or concealment, but it also tended to distract male visitors. Mina's slender figure, fashionably bobbed hair and merry light blue eyes made her, in the words of one admirer, "too attractive for her own good." To make matters more titillating, it was rumored that it was not uncommon for her to hold sessions in the nude and, according to some, she was especially adept at manifesting ectoplasm from her vagina.

Dr. Crandon believed that his lovely wife was a "remarkable psychic instrument" and her took her abroad to build up a consensus of favorable opinion from European experts. One of these was Sir Arthur Conan Doyle, who declared her to be a "very powerful medium" and, he said, "the validity of her gifts was beyond all question." J. Malcolm Bird, from *Scientific American*, shared Doyle's opinion and wrote a series of articles extolling her virtues. It was Bird who gave her the name "Margery" in an effort to protect the Crandons' privacy. Under this name, her fame steadily grew.

By bringing Margery to the attention of *Scientific American*, Conan Doyle had inadvertently started the most controversial portion of her career. With the urging of Bird, the panel had deadlocked over whether or not genuine phenomena were occurring in Margery's presence. No one would commit to anything without Houdini's opinion, which was why Orson Munn brought him back into the investigation. Not everyone was happy about this. J. Malcolm Bird who (unbelievably, given his opinions about Margery to start with) had been assigned to observe, organize and record the investigations with Margery. Bird wanted Houdini disqualified from the panel and for this reason, started the investigations without him.

Meanwhile, Houdini traveled to Boston, anxious to see the medium for himself.

On July 23, Houdini called at the Crandon house at No. 10 Lime Street, leaving his disguises and tricks behind. He wanted to see Mina perform under the same circumstances that his colleagues had experienced. The medium, meanwhile, relished the idea of converting the notorious debunker to her cause. Some observers saw the séance as an acid test, not just of Margery's authenticity but of Spiritualism itself.

An obviously amused Mina Crandon looks on as J. Malcolm Bird is knocked to the floor by an allegedly spirit controlled panel during the early *Scientific American* sessions

Houdini and Munn booked rooms at the Copley Plaza Hotel, ignoring the offer that the Crandons had made for the two men to join the other members of the committee at their home. They did accept a dinner invitation from the couple, however, and found Dr. Crandon to be a gracious host and a fascinating conversationalist. Margery, as they had heard, was a beautiful woman -- attractive, sensuous and confident.

It was so hot that evening that the men -- Crandon, Houdini, Munn, Bird, and R.W. Conant, who worked in the committeeman Comstock's laboratory -- removed their coats in the upstairs séance room. Bird confessed to Houdini that the room itself had never been thoroughly examined. Harry immediately went to work to remedy this sloppy oversight. There was no door to be locked between the room and the hallway leading to the stairs. He inspected the séance props: a megaphone, a three-sided cabinet, a phonograph, which usually played Margery's favorite song "Souvenir" and a bell box. The fourteen-inch-long wooden box contained batteries and a bell. A slight tap on a lever on the top would complete an electrical circuit and the bell would ring.

Margery and the four men sat in chairs forming a circle. She asked them all to link hands with one another. The medium was seated between Houdini and her husband. Bird sat outside of the circle, his right hand clasped around the linked hands of Margery and the doctor. Margery's right foot was pressed against her husband's left foot and her left foot was pressed against Houdini's right foot. These body contacts were meant to prove that the medium's hands

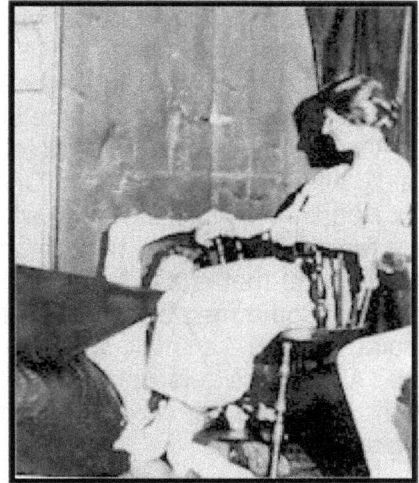

and feet were "under control" when the manifestations began.

Houdini watched as a spirit bell rang, a voice called out to him in the darkness, and a megaphone crashed to the floor at his feet. If these manifestations impressed him, he gave no sign of it. When the lights came back on, Houdini politely thanked his hosts and left.

On the drive back to the hotel, he finally spoke about what he was feeling. "I've got her," he said. "All fraud, every bit of it. One more sitting and I will be ready to expose everything."

Houdini was impressed by what he had seen at the Crandon home and very impressed with the famous Margery --- though not by her supernatural powers, he quickly assured Orson Munn. At his hotel that night, he explained how and why his conclusions about Margery differed from those of some members of the panel. One feat that had puzzled the panel was the ringing of a "spirit bell box," a small, wooden clapper-box that sounded an electric bell when pressed on the top. Although sitters on either side of her held Margery's hands, and her feet were in contact with theirs, the bell box rang many times during the séance, a happening that she attributed to Walter.

Usually, the bell box sat on the floor between Margery's legs, but Houdini had insisted that it be placed on the floor at his own feet. Regardless, the bell rang repeatedly. Houdini had a ready answer for this: "I had rolled my right trouser leg up above my knee. All that day, I had word a silk rubber bandage around that leg, just below the knee. By night, the part of the leg below the bandage had become swollen and painfully tender, thus giving me a much keener sense of feeling and making it easier to notice the slightest sliding of Mrs. Crandon's ankle or flexing of her muscles... I could distinctly feel her ankle slowly and spasmodically sliding as it pressed against mine while she gained space to raise her foot off the floor and touch the top of the box." In other words, Margery's foot, and not a spirit, had been responsible for the ringing of the bell.

Another of the evening's mysteries had involved a megaphone that, according to the spectral voice of Walter, had levitated in the air above the sitter's heads. Walter commanded that Houdini tell him where to throw the object and the magician instructed him to toss it in his direction. Moments later, the megaphone crashed to the floor in front of him. Houdini had an explanation for this, too. Earlier in the evening, when one of Margery's hands was free, she had snatched up the megaphone and had placed it on her head like a dunce cap. In the total darkness of the séance room, no one could have seen her do this. She later made the megaphone fly across the room by simply snapping her head forward. Houdini said: "This is the slickest ruse that I have ever seen..."

The next day, Houdini and Munn returned to Lime Street. In the séance room, alone with the publisher, he demonstrated that his explanations were practical.

In the wake of the first séance, Houdini refused to speak publicly about Margery. He did not reveal his opinions over what had occurred that night. Instead, he asked that more stringent tests be performed. It was rumored that Margery had somehow outwitted Houdini. Rumors also flew that perhaps her powers were genuine after all. Houdini ignored the rumors. He was convinced that he knew the truth.

That night, the tests were resumed in Dr. Comstock's apartment at the Charlesgate Hotel. His secretary, Gladys Wood, searched Margery before the séance and made a statement: "She removed most of her clothes and I examined her and them carefully. She wore a loose green linen dress into the séance room and I examined this carefully before she put it on. She also removed her shoes, and I examined her feet and shoes carefully. She then put her shoes on again. She also took down her hair, which I searched."

Dr. Comstock sat outside the circle recording his observations with a Dictaphone. The events began at 8:45 p.m. Walter's voice called for a card table to be substituted for the heavy table around which the circle had been formed. The card table was put into place with the bell box on top of it.

Background music was supplied by a phonograph and Dr. Comstock noted when it was started and stopped. The first manifestation in the darkened room was the movement of the threefold screen that had been set up behind Margery. At the end of the séance, it was found closed and flat, but still standing upright.

MARGERY GENUINE, SAYS CONAN DOYLE; HE SCORES HOUDINI

MEDIUM AND HER NEW CHAMPION

CRITICIZES THE EXPERT BODY IN SEVERE TERMS

Bell box and Carrington Derelict in Silence Under Attack

HE ANALYZES ALL EVIDENCE ADDUCED

Surprised American Gesticllation Should Tolerate Wizard's Conduct

The card table eerily tipped in the dark and fell toward Houdini, but it never fell completely over. At 9:45 p.m., it finally lurched over sideways, spilling the bell box to the floor. At 10:07, the bell box was put, at Walter's suggestion, between Houdini's feet. At 10:12, the bell rang shrilly three times. Walter shouted for Munn to straighten up. The publisher admitted that he had been bending over. Walter instructed Munn to tell the bell how many times it should rang and it chimed five times at his suggestion. Walter bid the sitters good night and the séance was abruptly over.

Dr. Comstock, Houdini, Munn and Bird went to another room to discuss the events that had occurred. Houdini said that he had released his grip on Munn's hand in the dark and had reached under the table when it was tilting. He felt Margery's hand underneath the table, lifting it. He had quickly pulled his hand away and reached for Munn's ear in the dark. He leaned over and whispered, "Shall I denounce and expose her now?" The publisher whispered back that he should wait.

Houdini, who had rolled up his trouser leg again, revealed that Margery's stocking had caught on the garter of his right stocking. When she complained that the buckle was hurting her, he had unfastened it. After that, he could feel her leg moving as it extended toward the bell box.

Harry was all for calling the newspapers immediately and exposing Margery as a fraud. The other men voted him down.

Munn and Houdini took the night train to New York. Bird stayed on as the Crandons' guest. During the trip, Munn told Harry that the September issue of the magazine had already gone to press, carrying an article by Bird praising Margery's mediumship. Houdini advised him to stop the presses. When the public learned that Margery was a fraud, the article would be embarrassing to the prestigious magazine. At first, Munn objected to the cost of remaking the issue, but he finally agreed to do it and the Bird article was removed.

Houdini was not the only member of the committee bothered by Bird's actions and writings. Dr. Walter Franklin Prince was also disturbed by Bird's early articles in *Scientific American* lauding Margery's gifts. He and Houdini were even more annoyed by his statements to the press. Bird was not a committee member, he was an employee of the magazine. Both men believed that the committee should be independent of the publication. They met with Munn and voiced their complaints.

Munn said that if Margery was using trickery, as Houdini claimed, the committee had to prove this to the public. Houdini was given the assignment of constructing a device that would prevent the medium from using her head, hands, and feet in the manner that he described.

Houdini with Margery, *Scientific American* publisher Orson Munn -- left -- and J. Malcolm Bird lurking in the background

Harry set about making plans for additional séances. To assure proper control at future sittings, Houdini designed a special "fraud preventer" cabinet, a crate with a slanted top that had openings at the top and sides for the medium's head and arms. Once inside, Margery's movements --- and her chances for deception --- would be severely limited. Reluctantly, Margery agreed to conduct the séance from inside the cabinet, but not before Houdini and Dr. Crandon exchanged such harsh words that they nearly came to blows. Dr. Crandon had earlier boasted to Sir Arthur Conan Doyle that he was willing to "crucify" any investigator who doubted his wife. Needless to say, Houdini was high on his list of potential victims.

J. Malcolm Bird offered to take Houdini's "fraud-preventer" to Boston

At left, Houdini in the "fraud-preventer" cabinet and above, Margery
attempts to conduct a sitting from inside of the box

in his car, but Harry, trusting no one, replied that he would transport it himself. He and Collins, his assistant, lugged it to Dr. Comstock's apartment early on the morning of August 25, 1924. It was an odd-shaped box that might have been a storage crate for an old-style roll top desk. There was ample room inside for the medium to sit comfortably on a chair. Semicircular holes were cut out of the hinged front and top panel so that when the cabinet was closed, a hole was created to circle the occupant's neck. Her hands were extended through holes in the cabinet sides so that committeemen could "control" them. Provision was also made for panels of wood to be nailed over the side openings should the committee wish to test her with her hands inside the box.

After the Crandons inspected the box, they withdrew and held a hasty conference. When they returned, the doctor insisted that Margery be allowed to try out in the device with her friends before she submitted to the committee's test. Reluctantly, the committee agreed.

The first séance with the cabinet was held behind closed doors as the investigators waited in another room. In thirty minutes, Dr. Crandon ushered his friends out and allowed the committee into the room. Bird, who was not present at the séance, wrote one version of what happened. Houdini, who was actually present, offered another. Both agreed that the sloped front of the box broke open in the dark. Dr. Crandon stated that Walter was responsible. Houdini said that Margery forced it open with her shoulders as it had only been held in place by two narrow strips of brass. With the front open, Margery could have leaned forward and reached the bell box, which was on a table in front of her, with her head.

The argument between Houdini and the Crandons became so heated that Walter's voice called out for peace and quiet. Margery's friends rushed into the room to replace the investigators and "psychic harmony" was temporarily restored. When the committee members were invited to return, Walter demanded to know how much Harry was being paid to stop the phenomena in the séance room. Houdini replied that he was actually losing money since he had to pass up a theater date in Buffalo to come to Boston for the séance. The séance then continued, but no manifestations were produced.

Eventually, Walter told Dr. Comstock to take the bell box under a light and examine it. Walter insisted that Houdini had done something to the bell so that it would not ring. An examination of the bell revealed that a piece of rubber had been wedged against the clapper, rendering it inoperable. Outraged, Dr. Crandon accused the magician of trying to sabotage the proceedings, a charge that Houdini repeatedly denied.

The committee members were angry. Even if he had not placed the rubber in the bell box, they stated that Houdini had not managed to build a "fraud-proof box" as he claimed he would do. Harry replied that he hadn't expected Margery to break out of it. He vowed that he would have the box in proper condition for the séance the next night.

As for the rubber wedge, he said Margery or her friends must have put it there to try and discredit him.

For the second séance, the box was heavily reinforced. Four staples, hasps and padlocks had been added. Unexpectedly, J. Malcolm Bird showed up for the session. Munn had told him to stay away from the hotel and Bird wanted to know why. Houdini and Dr. Prince were more than happy to enlighten him: Bird had given the Crandons information about the committee's findings in July and had also released unauthorized statements to the press. Before he was escorted from the hotel suite, he was allowed to formally resign as secretary for the committee.

Once again, Bird and Houdini told different stories about what occurred at the August 26 séance. Bird, who still believed in the authenticity of Margery's mediumship, but who was not present, said Houdini was satisfied by a search conducted by a woman of Margery's body and clothing. Houdini, on the other hand, wrote that he had objected to the superficial examination that was carried out. But Dr. Crandon would not permit a physician to be called for a more thorough inspection of his wife's anatomy.

The record of the séance was lacking in some important details. Apparently a pillow was placed under Margery's feet in the box, but it was not known who suggested this to be done or who actually put the pillow there.

Houdini held Margery's left hand as it was extended from the box. On the other side, Dr. Prince took her right hand. This was an important change as prior to this, Dr. Crandon had always controlled his wife's right hand. Harry repeatedly cautioned Dr. Prince not to release Margery's hand, not even for a moment.

Margery asked why he made such an issue of this. Harry replied, "I'll tell you, in case you have smuggled anything into the cabinet box you cannot conceal it as both your hands are secured and as far as they are concerned, you are helpless."

"Do you want to search me?" Margery asked.

"No, never mind, let it go," he replied. "I am not a physician."

Walter's voice sounded in the room. "Houdini, you are clever indeed, but it won't work."

Walter claimed that there was collapsible carpenter's ruler under the pillow on which Margery rested her feet. While Houdini had not been in the room just prior to the sitting, Walter said that his assistant had been, insinuating that Houdini arranged to have it hidden there. His voice became loud and abusive, "Houdini, you God damned bastard, get the hell out of here and never come back! If you don't, I will!"

The box was unlocked and a new carpenter's ruler, two feet long and folded into six-inch sections, was found tucked under the pillow. Dr. Comstock suggested that it had been left there when the box was being repaired. Orson Mull brought Collins into the room to be questioned. Collins said that his ruler was still in his pocket and he pulled it out to show them.

Houdini dictated a statement to the stenographer who was present: "I wish it recorded that I demanded Collins to take a sacred oath on the life of his mother that he did not put the ruler in the box and knew positively nothing about it. I also pledge my sacred word of honor as a man that the first I knew of the ruler in the box was when I was informed so by Walter."

In Houdini's opinion, the folding rule had been planted in the box in order to make him look bad. He swore that he had not put it there and the Crandons denied they were responsible. They blamed Houdini for the ruler and he blamed them. He resented anyone that would take their word --- and especially the word of Walter, the spirit guide --- over his.

No one knows how the ruler ended up in the box. In his biography of Houdini, author William Lindsay Gresham quoted Collins as admitting, years later, that he had hidden the ruler in the box on Houdini's instructions. The source of the story, although not given by Gresham, was Fred Keating, a magician who had been a guest of the Crandons in the house on Lime Street at the time Hereward Carrington was investigating the medium. Keating, however, was biased against Houdini. Several days before Gresham interviewed him, Keating had seen an unpublished manuscript in which Houdini, while praising Keating as a magician, commented in unflattering terms about Keating's skills as a psychical investigator. Author Milbourne Christopher believed that the story of Collins' so-called confession was sheer fiction.

Unfortunately, the investigators did not thoroughly rule out all possibilities of fraud. If the ruler had been taken to a laboratory for analysis, fingerprints might have been found to show who had last handled it. The *Scientific American* committee, however, was not that scientific.

On the day of the third and final August séance, Munn, Prince, Houdini and the Crandons had dinner together. Houdini later wrote that Margery said she had heard he planned to denounce her from the stage of Keith's Theater. If he did, she said, her friends would give him a thrashing. She didn't want her son to read someday that his mother was a fraud.

Houdini, who usually had a soft spot for mothers, was unmoved by her words. "Then don't be a fraud," he told her.

Dr. Comstock brought a medium-control device of his own that night. It was a shallow wooden box into which Margery and an investigator, sitting face-to-face, put their feet. A board was locked in place over their knees. The sides of the box were open, except at the bottom and top so the restraint wouldn't interfere with a "psychic structure." When the medium's hands were held, and the bell box was on the floor by the box, she was under excellent control.

According to Houdini's account, while the committee waited for the bell to ring and other manifestations to occur, Dr. Crandon turned to him and spoke, "Some day, Houdini, you will see the light, and if it were to occur this evening, I would gladly give $10,000 to charity."

Harry replied, "It may happen, but I doubt it."

The doctor repeated. "If you were converted this evening I would willingly give $10,000 to charity."

Dr. Comstock's fraud control was effective. When Margery's hands were held by someone other than her husband, and while her hands and feet were immobilized, no spirit phenomena was produced. Nothing occurred that night.

Houdini had not been converted and Dr. Crandon still had his $10,000.

The aftermath of the Margery séances was troubling for everyone involved. There were many, including some of the committee, who believed that Houdini had been the one who was caught cheating this time. He was widely discredited for it, leading some to doubt the integrity of some of his earlier investigations. In any case, *Scientific American* finally declined to grant the prize to Margery, in large part because of Houdini's exposure. The confrontational magician had quarreled, often violently, with every member of the committee. J. Malcolm Bird, whom Houdini suspected of active collusion with the Crandons, was angry with the magician and he continued to insist Harry should have been disqualified at the very beginning.

Houdini further outraged Bird, the Crandons and their supporters when he published a small book called "Houdini Exposes the Tricks Used by the Boston Medium Margery." He was adamant about the fact that Margery was doing nothing more than offering clever tricks. In his final verdict on the medium, he wrote: "My decision is, that everything which took place at the séances which I attended was a deliberate and conscious fraud..."

From the other side, Walter chimed in his final words about Houdini. He ended them with a prediction: Houdini would be dead within a year. Houdini managed to defy this prophecy, but not by much. He died in 1926 and in an interview with the press, Margery had only good things to say about the magician, praising him for his virile personality and great determination.

Despite Houdini's exposure, Margery emerged from the debacle relatively unscathed. She continued her séances and by the end of 1924, she had begun to produce even greater manifestations, including "spirit arms" that rang the bell box and caused objects to fly about in the séance room. This "teleplasmic"

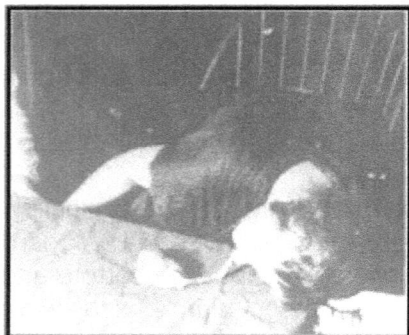

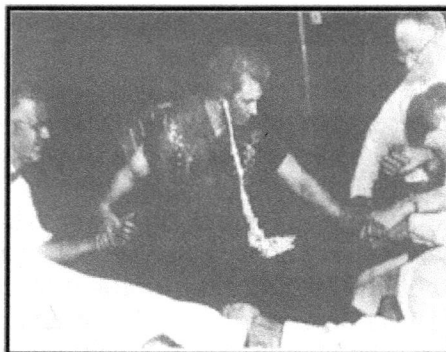

After the controversy with Houdini, Margery continued to perform as a medium. In the photos above, she is seen blowing masses of ectoplasm from her nose and ear during different sessions.

manifestation was similar to that produced by the famous Italian medium, Eusapia Palladino.

In 1925, J. Malcolm Bird published a book that supported Margery and as the research officer of the American Society for Psychical Research, he was able to sway many other ASPR members to her side. They became her greatest supporters and devoted hundreds of pages in the ASPR journal to her séances.

Eric J. Dingwall, an officer of the Society for Psychical Research in England, read of his American colleagues' support, and decided to investigate the medium for himself. He wanted to see the ectoplasm that Margery was manifesting and Dr. Crandon allowed him to view it by the light of a red lamp, which Crandon flashed on and off to reveal quick glances at the phenomenon. Too much light, Dr. Crandon said, would have an inhibiting effect on the mysterious material, said to be the manifestation of spirit emanations. Dingwall wrote to a friend: "The materialized hands are connected by an umbilical cord to the medium. They seize upon objects and displace them. Later, when he was permitted to grasp one of the "ghost hands," he described it as feeling like "a piece of cold raw beef or possibly a piece of soft, wet rubber."

Halfway through his investigations, Dingwall began having doubts. Dr. Crandon's red lamp never allowed him to see the ectoplasm actually emanating from Margery's body. He had only seen it after the fact. Odder still, many of the photographs revealed that a large number of the emanations seemed to be hanging from slender, almost invisible threads. Others who looked at the photos said that the "hands" looked suspiciously like animal lung tissue, a substance that Dr. Crandon could have

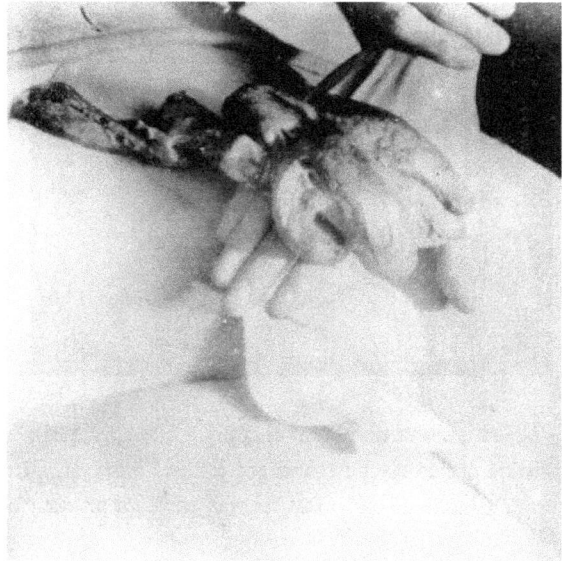

Margery also continued her reputation for holding sexually charged seances. In this photograph of Margery's vagina -- discreetly covered by a handkerchief -- it is seen to exude a dark-colored ectoplasm.

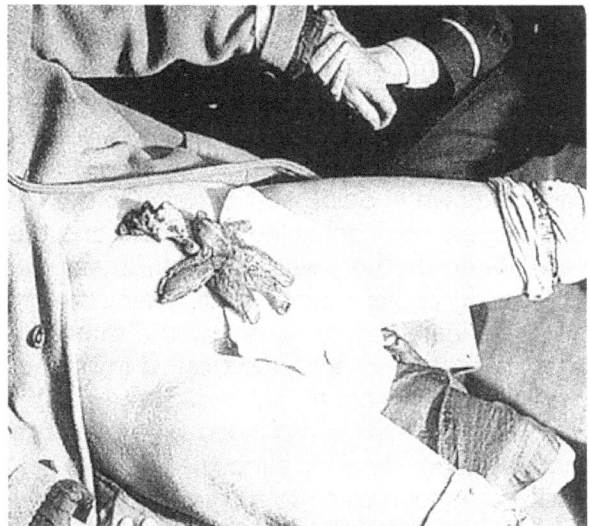

Another photo of Margery with her dress raised and her stockings rolled down, against exuding ectoplasm from her vagina.

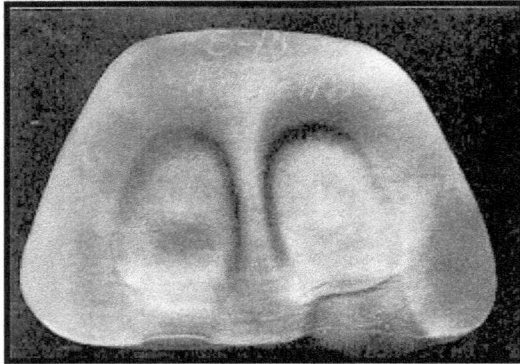

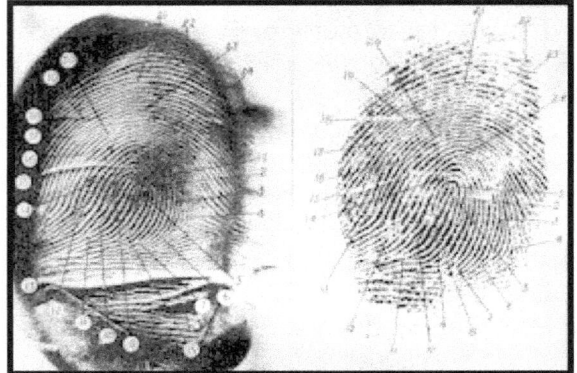

At left is a wax thumbprint allegedly left by spirit guide, Walter, during one of Margery's sessions. This "physical evidence" of the afterlife stunned many followers and psychical investigators. However, the fingerprint analysis at left, arranged by E.E. Dudley, proved that the wax prints did not come from Walter -- but from the Crandons' dentist!

obtained through his work at Boston hospitals. Dingwall's final report on the case was inconclusive.

As usual, Margery was unconcerned. Sitters continued to file into the séance room at the Crandons' Lime Street home. One investigation after another raised allegations of fraud but no one was ever able to make the accusations stick. Even J.B. Rhine, who would later become one the largest personalities in paranormal research, was intrigued by Margery but was unimpressed with what he saw. As always, though, Conan Doyle defended the medium and when Rhine published an unflattering account of his experiences with Margery, Doyle bought space in several Boston newspapers to run a reply. The black-bordered message read simply: "J.B. Rhine is an ass."

In 1928, Margery began to develop a highly unusual manifestation that made her even more widely known in Spiritualist circles. On the table in front of her during a séance would be placed two dishes, one containing hot water and the other cold. In the first dish was a piece of dental wax. When the wax was softened, it was claimed that her spirit guide, Walter, would make an impression of his thumb on it. Then, the thumbprint was put into cold water to harden. The prints appeared mysteriously on the same night that Margery obtained the wax from her dentist. A so-called fingerprint expert called in by the Crandons stated that the thumbprint matched one that was taken from an old razor that once belonged to Walter Stinson.

Margery had confounded the skeptics and believers were enthralled by this new manifestation. It was almost as if the spirit was leaving a calling card, even better. The excitement soon came to a crashing end, however.

Psychic researcher E.E. Dudley set out to compare Walter's wax print with those belonging to regulars at the Crandon séances and made a surprising discovery: Walter's thumbprint was identical in every way to that of Margery's dentist, Dr. Frederick Caldwell. Someone had apparently used a sample thumbprint that Dr. Caldwell made for Margery to create a metal die-stamp that was suitable for making impressions in wax.

This was the end of the ruse. Many of Margery's most devoted followers drifted away. J. Malcolm Bird, once her staunchest defender, admitted that, at times, he had been guilty of elaborations and half-truths about Margery's so-called "wonders." Even Conan Doyle was strangely quiet. The scientific community let it be known that Margery's séances were no longer of interest.

Margery's decline was quick and tragic. After the death of Dr. Crandon in 1939, Mina grew depressed and turned to alcohol for consolation. She began to look older than her years, gained weight and watched as her beauty faded away. She continued to hold séances, finding people who still believed in her, and during one sitting, she grew so distraught that she climbed to the roof of her home and threatened to throw herself off. She died at the age of fifty-four in 1941.

Many researchers today believe that some elements of the paranormal were present in Crandon's séances, but just what was genuine and what was not remain unknown. Crandon and her husband were known for baiting investigators and trying to fool them if possible. The Crandons simply never seemed to care who believed them and who did not. Just what secrets did Mina Crandon hold? We'll never know; she took them with her to her grave.

THE CRUSADE CONTINUES

Houdini quickly recovered from the accusations that were thrown his way after the *Scientific American* investigations. Throughout the rest of 1924, he embarked on another nationwide lecture tour, blasting the fraudulent mediums that he was trying to drive out of business. The tour took him to small towns where he had never played before and to big cities where he was a vaudeville favorite. His contract paid him $1,500 per week, plus transportation, although in the larger cities he received fifty percent of the net receipts. His contract specified that the words "hocus" and "fakery" were not to be used in advertisements. He considered them "too vulgar."

In Denver, Harry was challenged by the Reverend Josie Stewart, who had been exposed as a fraud in New York by the *Scientific American* committee. She wanted to take the stage and prove to her hometown audience that she was the real thing. She specialized in spirit messages that mysteriously appeared on previously blank cards. The cards that had been given to her by the committee had been secretly identified with pinpricks. When the spirit writing appeared, the pinpricks vanished, proving, the committee charged, that the medium had switched cards. Now, in Denver, Houdini stated that he would give her the entire night's receipts if she could produce any alleged spirit phenomena that he couldn't duplicate. She produced no manifestations, but she put up quite a verbal battle, during which her followers got into a fistfight with Houdini's supporters. The next day, the *Denver Post* ran a story headlined, "Houdini Starts a Riot."

In San Jose, California, Houdini visited the unique house that had been built by Sarah Lockwood Winchester, the widow of the Winchester arms magnate. Describing the visit, Houdini wrote, "Her spirit guide told her that as long as she kept adding onto the house, she would live. For thirty-six years, she kept building and building. I walked through the house at midnight with Mrs. Houdini and know that she will never think we live in a big house. Mrs. Winchester built 160 rooms. There are over 200 doors, 10,000 windows, over 150,000 panes of glass. Some of the windows must have cost over $2,000. There are forty-seven fireplaces, one room especially built

The Winchester Mystery House

to hold a séance has a wardrobe in which she had different colored robes and whenever she wished to talk to any particular spirit, she would don the colored robe required... It was the greatest house I ever saw, meaning it is the largest dwelling ever built."

Legend had it that Houdini was one of the only visitors ever allowed in the house by the reclusive Sarah Winchester but this is merely part of the mysterious house's lore. Sarah Winchester's recipe for immortality didn't work. She had died in her sleep in 1922, four years before Houdini came to see the house.

Houdini returned to Boston for the first time since the Margery debacle in January 1925. He gave the city's mayor $5,000 in bonds as photographers took pictures. The bonds were to be awarded to any medium, Margery included, who was able to produce physical phenomena that Houdini could not reproduce. Symphony Hall, where Sir Arthur Conan Doyle had once presented lectures endorsing Spiritualism, was filled to capacity for Houdini's performance. Occupying one hundred chairs on the crowded stage was a committee Houdini invited as his guests: ministers, reporters, magicians and well-known local citizens.

This was a Houdini that was unfamiliar to Bostonians, who had often seem him perform at Keith's. He was a bit stockier, his once-dark curly hair was now thinner and laced with gray and his demeanor was more serious. His bright, hypnotic eyes remained the same, however. He spoke slowly, making his words very clear. He had no intention of attacking anyone's religion, he said. Everyone should be allowed to worship as he or she saw fit, as long as they remained within the laws of the country and did not hurt anyone.

Houdini stated that he was not a skeptic. He longed to believe in the spirit world and more than anything else, he longed for some word from his late, beloved mother -- or from any of the friends with whom he had made pacts before they died. His enemies, he complained, dismissed him as a mere magician, a showman. But he had spent nearly thirty-five years studying

Spiritualism and had investigated scores of mediums. Like his father, he was a scholar. He had an immense library in New York, one of the largest in the world on witchcraft and magic. Anyone could talk to the dead, he told the audience, but as far as he could tell, the dead did not answer. Inmates of lunatic asylums heard strange voices and saw phantoms, but this did not make them real. Millions of dollars had been spent on psychical research without producing any solid results. Since 1854, Harvard University had a standing offer of $500 for any genuine case of mediumship. That very day, Houdini reminded them, he had given $5,000 to the mayor with instructions to award it to any authentic medium in the city of Boston -- but there had been no takers. Not even from the same mediums who regularly demonstrated their manifestations, under their own fixed conditions, to their followers for a dollar or two.

Men like Sir Oliver Lodge and Sir Arthur Conan Doyle were menaces to mankind, Houdini firmly stated, eliciting a gasp from the audience. They were great men and deserved to be respected in their fields, but were not qualified to say that mediums they knew of were genuine. Most of these so-called "psychics" were nothing more than escape artists and thieves. Houdini could perform feats of phony spirit phenomena that would defy scientific explanation, but it was nothing more than trickery. He even confessed to posing as a medium himself, as a foolish and poverty-stricken young man, and told how he had faked a message from a murdered man in Kansas that caused a panic in a theater.

He showed the audience a letter from Lady Emily Shackleton, widow of Sir Ernest Shackleton, who died in the Antarctic of a heart attack aboard his ship *Quest* in 1922. The letter denied that Conan Doyle could have heard from the late explorer. Harry told of Lady Doyle in Atlantic City writing page after page of messages that supposedly came from his dead mother. Cecilia, who had been educated in Europe, could speak five languages, but very little English. Sir Arthur, when he learned this from Houdini, had laughingly asserted that his mother had gone to college in heaven and had learned English.

After this lengthy introduction, the house lights were turned off and slides of famous mediums like the Fox sisters and the Davenport brothers appeared on screen. Houdini summarized their careers and explained how their feats were mere tricks, not the result of psychic powers. After the lights came back up, Houdini demonstrated how the mediums performed their fraudulent activities. A man from the audience was invited onto the stage and Houdini had him sit down at a table, like one that would have been used in séance, and had him examine a slate that Harry gave to him. The slate was blank but after the man held it under the table, writing appeared on it. A medium, Houdini told the audience, would call this a spirit message -- but it wasn't. He showed how he had switched slates under his chair before the man grasped the slate beneath the table. The audience howled with laughter.

Houdini then launched into his version of events in the Margery case, stunning the audience as he explained how he had discovered the trickery that occurred during her séances. Two spectators were invited to the stage, sitting on either side of him. Both had their heads covered with hoods to simulate the dark conditions of the séance room. Each man held one of Houdini's hands, each controlled one of his feet. Houdini asked one of the men if a megaphone was sitting on the floor next to him. The man reached out his hand, touched the megaphone, said that it was there and took Houdini's hand again. He told the men to stretch back in their chairs and they did.

He bent forward, put his head under the table in front of him and lifted it so that only two of the legs were on the floor. Then he pulled his head back and the "levitated" table thumped back into place. The audience once again laughed loudly. "That's exactly how Margery did it," he exclaimed.

Once more, Harry asked the man on his right to make sure the megaphone was next to him. The man again released his hand and verified the position of the trumpet. In the few seconds this action took, Houdini picked up the megaphone as soon as the man's hand left it, jammed it on his head and had his hand ready for the spectator to take hold of it again. Neither of the volunteers was aware that anything out of the ordinary had occurred. The man to Houdini's left was told that the megaphone was floating through the air above his head. Did he wish for it to fall near him? The man said that he did and so Harry turned in his direction and with a shake of his head, made the megaphone fall into the hooded volunteer's lap. The audience broke into gales of laughter once more.

Houdini demonstrated how the bell box on the table could be rung with his forehead while his hands and feet were held in place. The enclosure that he had built for Margery was brought on stage, the first time it had been seen in Boston since the controversial series of séances. He told about Walter and showed how "spirit hands" were made and how, using a long tong-like device, they could touch the faces of séance attendees sitting some distance away. He invited another man up from the audience and the man sat at one end of a table with Houdini at the other. The man put his feet on Houdini's under the table and held Houdini's hands across the top. A dinner bell rang under the table. A tambourine jangled. Control had not been broken, the volunteer insisted, he could still feel Harry's hands and feet. Houdini's assistant lifted the cloth over the table and the audience laughed. The man's feet were still on Houdini's shoes, but Harry had slipped out of the right one. He was able to grab the bell with his toes and as he shook the foot, the bell rang.

After taking questions from the audience, Houdini closed down the show. It had been a resounding success and it was repeated over and over again across the country. The show cast him in three roles: magician, escapologist and debunker of mediums. The shows sold out everywhere and Houdini found himself   extending tour dates because the demand for tickets was so high. Reporters from newspapers in the cities he played joined his corps of psychic investigators, which until then had consisted of his wife; Julia Sawyer, Bess' twenty-two-year-old niece; his stage assistants, friends and fellow magicians. Eventually, he even hired private detectives who devoted their time to the task of exposing spirit fraud.

During an engagement in Cleveland, Harry, wearing shabby clothes and thick glasses as a disguise, went with County Prosecutor Edward B. Stanton and reporter Louis B. Seltzer to the home of medium George Renner on Superior Avenue. In his séance room on the second floor, the medium showed his clients four spirit photographs. Houdini's name was mentioned and Renner called the magician a fraud. "I once paid two and a half dollars to see him," Renner said. "He's a big frost and a faker. They chased him out of Massachusetts. When he says Spiritualism is a fake, he lies, folks. Tonight we will prove that Spiritualism is genuine and Houdini is a faker."

Three other visitors, not members of Houdini's group, joined the circle around a large table. Renner instructed them to place their hands on the knees of the persons on either side of them, checking to make sure his instructions were carried out. Then he turned to Seltzer, Houdini's reporter friend, and said, "Young man, you look a little frightened. There is no need to be. If the spirits brush your cheek, don't be afraid. If the guitar or trumpet floats over your head, keep quiet. They will not harm you."

The medium stood at the end of the table and announced, "Folks, you will hear tonight from Jimmy Nolan of Anderson, Wisconsin. Are you ready?" Renner fastened two frames covered with opaque paper to the windows, then draped rugs over the three doors to the room. He took his seat in the circle and switched off the lights, plunging the room into darkness. It was not long before a booming voice broke the silence, announcing that it was "Jimmy."

There were raps, a voice claiming to be the father of one of the sitters, and that of an Indian chief. Then the guitar began to play, apparently floating around the room in the darkness. It returned to the table and after the music stopped, the lights were turned on again. Renner was in his seat, his hands on the knees of those next to him, as they had been earlier.

Rising to leave, Seltzer said that he wanted to pay for himself and his two friends. Renner accepted the $3 but protested that the séance had only just started. Once more the room was darkened. A spirit voice sang "Nearer My God to Thee" and "Jerusalem" and the sitters joined in. A whooshing sound indicated that the trumpets were now hovering above the table. They clanked as they dropped back to the table. A flashlight was switched on and a bright light was suddenly trained on the medium. He blinked his eyes. His hands were covered with soot and there were dark streaks on his face.

Houdini's voice called out, "Mr. Renner, you are a fraud. Your hands are full of lampblack. The trumpets are also full of lampblack. That's how you got it on your hands."

Reporter Seltzer switched on the lights and Houdini explained how he had taken a can of lampblack from his pocket in the dark and coated the trumpet with it.

Renner shouted angrily. "I have been a medium for forty years and I have never been exposed!"

Houdini smirked, "Well, you are now."

"Who are you?" Renner demanded to know.

"My name," said the shabby little man, removing his glasses, "is Houdini." He then introduced the county prosecutor and Seltzer, whose story appeared on the front page of the *Cleveland Press* the next day.

Renner was arrested, tried and found guilty of obtaining money under false pretenses. He was fined $25 and sentenced to spend six months in jail.

In Pittsburgh, the Reverend Alice S. Dooley, of the Pittsburgh Church of Divine Healing, volunteered to be tested at the Alvin Theater in September. Harry sealed three questions in envelopes and hung them on a string suspended across the stage. The psychic asked for music to put her in the mood so that she could commune with her astral influences. The orchestra obliged with a slow waltz.

She pointed to the first envelope. "All is well. March 30, 1894," she said.

No vibrations were produced by the second envelope.

Her answer to the third was, "It is possible."

The committee of judges and three clergymen opened the first envelope. The question was, "What Pittsburgh chief of police did I meet in Europe? When, how and where?" The psychic's reply had not answered any part of Houdini's query. The date she had given was meaningless. He had not gone to Europe until 1900.

The third question was, "What was the name of the Hindu who taught me the East Indian Needle Trick? Where and what year and the circumstances?" Her reply of "it was possible," was scarcely a answer at all.

The critic in the *Cincinnati Commercial Tribune* wrote that the show "was good fun from start to finish... Houdini manages these magical shows just a bit better than anyone else.. There's one big difference between Houdini on a vaudeville bill and Houdini in his own show. In the latter instance, there's more of him. Ergo, the show is better."

During a week in Syracuse, Julia Sawyer and Rose Mackenberg, one of Harry's assistants, went on a special mission to Lily Dale, the famous Spiritualist summer camp. At Lily Dale, the curious could patronize clairvoyants, message-readers, and various physical mediums. Many believers spent their vacations there. In 1916, the Fox family farmhouse, where Kate and Maggie Fox had started producing the phenomena that gave birth to the Spiritualist movement, was moved to the Lily Dale grounds. Séances continued to be held in the house.

Julia masqueraded as a curious teenager and Rose as a housewife. For $3 each, a medium named Pierre Keeler admitted them to a slate séance. Keeler produced a spirit message for Julia from a sister she never had, as well as communication from her mother and brother, who were said to be happy in the spirit world. This was quite a shock to Julia since they were both still alive. After the séance, Keeler was taken to meet Julia's elderly uncle, who sat slumped in a wheelchair under the care of a nurse. The "elderly uncle" was actually Houdini, who whipped off his disguise and announced that he had the goods on Keeler. The medium admitted his deceptions. He and Houdini, Keeler pleaded, were in the same business.

"Not so, "Harry replied, "I'm a legitimate entertainer, you're a cheat."

The "nurse" who witnessed the exchange was actually a reporter for a Syracuse newspaper.

When Houdini began his run on Broadway at the 44th Street Theater, the year that Walter, Margery's spirit voice, had given him to live was almost over. Only one time -- when he came down with a cold on Halloween 1925 -- had he even been under a doctor's care. For a man who was nearly fifty-two years old, he was in amazing physical condition.

Houdini played in Brooklyn and Manhattan and then traveled to Hartford, Connecticut, for an engagement. It was snowing when he arrived and he went straight from the station to speak before four hundred men at the Advertising Club. He then addressed a radio audience on WTIC. Hundreds were in line in front of the theater an hour before the show. Despite the storm, the house was sold out when the curtain went up.

During Houdini's three-week run in Philadelphia, he took the night train to Washington. On

Houdini with Senator Arthur Capper. Houdini had endorsed anti-fortune-telling legislation in Washington in 1924. Neither the bill proposed to a Senate Committee nor the one considered by the House passed.

the morning of February 26, 1926, he testified before a House of Representatives committee in support of bill H.R. 8989, which would ban fortune telling in the District of Columbia. This bill, and two similar ones introduced in the Senate, had the magician's complete approval.

The Spiritualists, their associations and publications were as vehemently against the bills as Houdini was in favor of them. The room where the Subcommittee on Judiciary of the Committee on the District of Columbia held their public hearing was jammed. Among the spectators were Spiritualists, as well as palm readers, crystal gazers, and clairvoyants.

Houdini addressed the committee: "Please understand that, emphatically, I am not attacking a religion. I respect every genuine believer in Spiritualism or any other religion. But this thing they call Spiritualism, wherein a medium intercommunicates with the dead, is a fraud from start to finish. There are only two kinds of medium, those who are mental degenerates and who ought to be under observation, and those who are deliberate cheats and frauds. I would not believe a fraudulent medium under oath; perjury means nothing to them.

"How can you call it a religion when you get men and women in a room together and they feel each other's hands and bodies? The inspirational mediums are not quite as bad as that. But they guess and by "fishing" methods and by reading obituary notices they get the neurotics to believe that they heard voices and see forms. In thirty-five years, I have never seen one genuine medium."

Washington abounded with fortune-tellers, lucky charm sellers, card readers and mediums of every kind, Houdini claimed. For $25, anyone could buy a clairvoyant license, then point to it and say: "If I were not genuine, I could not get a license."

Harry repeated his offer of $10,000 for proof of mediumship. He took a telegram from his pocket, crumpled it and threw it on the table. He dramatically looked back at the audience. "Read that, you clairvoyant mediums, and show me up. Tell me the contents of that telegram." The Spiritualists remained silent.

Representative Frank Reid, a Republican from Illinois, broke in: "I will tell you what it says --

please send more money."

Houdini replied: "You can make your own deductions. You are not a clairvoyant."

"Oh yes, I am," Reid quipped, setting off a round of laughter.

Houdini smiled and crumpled up another telegram and tossed it on the table. "All right, if you're a clairvoyant, tell me what this wire is."

"It is asking if it didn't come," Reid said.

Houdini shook his head. "No, sir. Everyone guesses at it."

Although these statements came from the official proceedings of the committee, newspapers gave varying accounts of what occurred that day. Different statements were given as to what Representative Reed said and some even claimed that he jumped out of his seat shouting, "That's an invitation to you to appear before the committee this morning. I win the $10,000!"

The *New York Morning Telegraph* account included an incident that was not mentioned anywhere else. When Houdini challenged any of the mediums in the room to tell him the name his mother called him before he was born, a palmist, standing just outside the door, was said to have remarked, "She probably called him an incipient damn fool."

Jane B. Coates, one of Washington's best-known mediums, took the stand. She was asked to define the term mystic. "A mystic, "she replied, "is a person who has evoluted [sic] certain senses within themselves which bring them knowledge from the world beyond. A congressman asked her if Houdini was a mystic. Mrs. Coates replied, "I think Mr. Houdini is one of the greatest mystics in the world today." The hearing was adjourned until May 18.

When the session resumed, Houdini returned to Washington to be the star witness for the bill's supporters. For three days, he attacked the mediums and they lashed back at him when they took the stand. Harry showed how he could produce a "spirit" voice form a trumpet without moving his lips and caused a message to appear on a pair of blank slates. When the Spiritualists called him "vile" and "crazy," he asked Bess to come forward.

Harry said to her, "I want the chairman to see you... On June 22, 1926, we celebrate our thirty-second anniversary. There are no medals and no ribbons on me, but when a girl will stick to a man for thirty-two years as she did, and when she will starve with me and work with me through thick and thin, it is a pretty good recommendation. Outside of my great mother, Mrs. Houdini has been my greatest friend. Have I ever shown traces of being crazy, unless it was about you?"

"No," Bess quietly replied.

"Am I brutal to you or vile?"

"No."

"Am I a good boy?"

"Yes."

"Thank you, Mrs. Houdini."

The hearings ended on May 21. Despite Houdini's testimony, and best efforts, no bill to ban fortune telling was ever passed.

During the eight weeks that Houdini performed at the Princess Theater in Chicago, his staff investigated more than forty mediums in the Windy City. Eight of the nineteen sitters with Mrs. Minnie Reichart one evening were members of Houdini's team. In the dark séance room, spirit voices sang such divergent songs as "Nearer My God to Thee" and "Yes Sir, That's my Baby."

Aware that Houdini was in town, Mrs. Reichart unplugged the only lamp in the room. Even if someone tried to turn on the wall switch, no lights would interrupt the séance. Her spirit control, Chief Blackhawk, was speaking through her spirit trumpet in a guttural tone when a flash illuminated the room. A Chicago American photographer had taken a picture. One man pulled up the shade and another threw open a window, which was the quickest exit route. Five men jumped to the lawn outside. The séance room had been plunged into chaos.

"Where's the outlet for the floor socket?" someone shouted.

A female voice screamed, "Don't put on the lights. Do you want to kill our medium?"

Mrs. Reichart's supporters rushed Houdini's crew out of the house. The medium's sister slapped the photographer, knocking off his hat. Another swing sent the flash equipment tumbling from his hand onto the grass. He clutched his camera firmly in his other fist and fought his way to his car. His hat, his camera case and his flashgun were lost in the scuffle.

The photographic plate was developed in the newspaper darkroom. The single shot had captured the plump medium holding the trumpet to her lips with a handkerchief-wrapped hand so no fingerprints would appear on the shiny surface. The photograph, four columns wide, titled "Picture Bares Fraud," appeared on the front page of the March 11 issue of the *Chicago American*.

The lengthy run in Chicago produced one unexpected event when Harry was visited in his dressing room by an elderly couple, Mr. and Mrs. Ernest Benninghofen. They complimented him on his exposures of fraudulent mediums and Mrs. Benninghofen explained that she had once been known as Anna Clark, the "mother medium," because she had developed so many young psychics, including Mrs. Cecil Cook, then a leading figure in the movement. Twenty years before, Mrs. Benninghofen had sold Mrs. Cook her North Side apartment and her list of wealthy suckers.

She told Harry, "When I reformed, I had no intention of going before the public and showing how tricks were done. I will come any time or any place to help you, as I now see the great good that is being done."

Harry was overwhelmed by the visit. He had an ally, ordained by the National Spiritualist Association, who would stand before an audience, confess her sins and demonstrate the feats that had fooled hundreds of those who had believed in her. He arranged a press conference at the Sherman Hotel and promised reporters one of his greatest revelations ever.

By coincidence, the twenty-seventh annual convention of the Illinois State Spiritualist Association was in progress on Chicago's West Side. During the convention, John Slater, who was said to have made over a million dollars with his séances, ridiculed Houdini's stage exposures.

At the Sherman Hotel, Houdini was busy introducing Mrs. Benninghofen to the press. He announced that she would showcase her entire repertoire. The lights were switched off and a prayer and song ushered in the "ghostly" phenomena. Trumpets rose and floated in the dark room. Ghostly hands appeared and disappeared. Spirits talked through the trumpets in the air, including a little girl named Rosie, a deep-voiced Uncle John, elderly Aunt Susan and even Chief Big Elk, a war-whooping Indian.

After astounding the reporters with her seemingly genuine antics, Mrs. Benninghofen began her exposures. Voices came at distances far beyond a trumpet length. She showed how she had attached two trumpets, mouthpiece to mouthpiece, in the dark. She whispered at one end of the trumpets and her voice came out of the far end of the other. She exhibited her vocal range, showing how she could speak in many voices and many tones, including those of a child and an Indian.

Houdini helped her unveil the secret of ghostly hands. A glove coated with luminous paint was glued to a piece of black cardboard. When the luminous side was turned toward the spectators, the hand appeared in the dark; when it was turned away, the hand vanished. By moving the cardboard quickly from one area to another, he produced what seemed to be two hands in different places. Mrs. Benninghofen confessed that she concealed the hand-producing device under her skirt.

She also demonstrated how she was able to free one of her hands in the dark, when the sitters on either side of her believed she was being controlled. She released her right hand momentarily, "to brush back her hair," and then clasped hands again with the man on her right. One this time, she clasped his hand with her left hand, which was held at the wrist by a man to her left. Neither man realized that one hand was being "controlled" rather than two. With her free hand, the medium could swing trumpets in the air, fit mouthpiece to mouthpiece, could speak through it and even tap people on the head at a distance with the end of the trumpet.

It was, as Houdini had promised, an amazing press conference.

The reformed spirit medium, Annie Benninghofen, appeared with Houdini in Chicago and explained to reporters how she had produced "spirit voices" from "floating" trumpets during her sittings.

Mrs. Benninghofen explained, "I really believed in Spiritualism all the time I was practicing it, but I thought I was justified in helping the spirits out. They couldn't float a trumpet around the room; I did it for them. They couldn't speak, so I spoke for them. I thought I was justified in trickery because through trickery I could get more converts to what I thought was a good and beautiful religion. When people asked me if the spirits really moved trumpets, I told them to judge for themselves. So while I acted a lie, I didn't tell one."

It was a shame, Houdini said, that more mediums could not say the same.

BURIED ALIVE

Houdini ended his season on the road in Harrisburg, Pennsylvania, in May 1926. He returned to New York with the intention of spending the summer months relaxing and devising new mysteries for his fall season.

Instead of relaxing, though, he was confronted with a new psychic sensation. Hereward Carrington, the only *Scientific American* committee member to continue endorsing Margery, began trumpeting about a new medium: the "Egyptian Miracle Man," Rahman Bey. The slender, bearded mystic claimed to be able to influence his body with his mind, slowing the pulse in one of his wrists while increasing it in the other, thrusting steel needles through his flesh, and resting with a sword blade under the back of his neck, with another under his heels, as a man holding a sledge hammer cracked a stone slab on his chest. As a climax to his show, he went into a trance and was buried in a coffin under a mound of sand. Carrington lectured for ten minutes on suspended animation and living burials, then the sand was shoveled away and Bey was removed from the coffin. He revived himself enough to walk unsteadily to the footlights and accept thunderous applause and curtain calls.

In July, Rahman Bey allowed himself to be enclosed in a metal box and instead of being buried in the sand, the coffin was immersed in the Hudson River. Bey announced that he would attempt to stay submerged in the coffin for an entire hour. Two doctors took his pulse count and measured his heartbeat. Bey pressed his fingertips to his temples, shut his eyes, and lowered his head. He swayed, fell backward into the arms of his assistants and they lifted him into a bronze coffin. The inner lid was bolted and the outer cover was soldered shut.

The coffin, lifted by a hoist, was swung over the water. Before it was lowered into the river, an electric alarm bell rang. The bell was part of a safety device controlled from inside the box. The hoist brought the coffin back and workmen feverishly hacked away at the cover, tearing away the lid with chisels, hammers and shears.

Nineteen minutes after Bey had been sealed into the coffin, he was lifted out. His body was

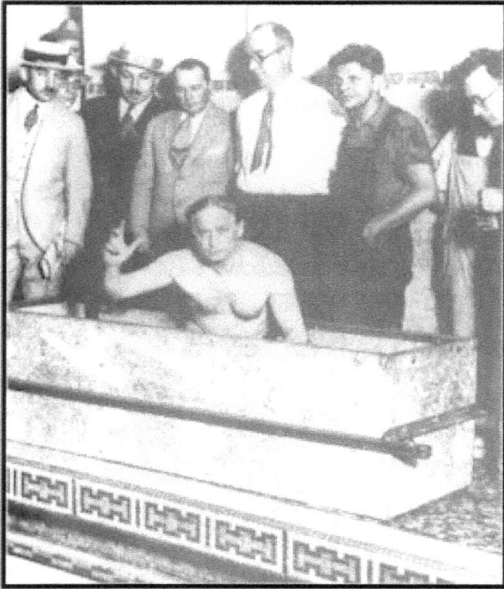

Houdini in his "coffin", just before his underwater stunt in the Shelton Hotel swimming pool

soaked with sweat and his face was twisted in a bizarre mask. After emerging from the trance, he explained, through an interpreter, that he had not rung the bell. Someone offered the theory that perhaps when the coffin had been lifted, his body had shifted against the buzzer and rang the bell.

Thirteen days later, he was ready to try the underwater stunt again. This time, the coffin was lowered into the waters of the Dalton Hotel swimming pool on 59th Street. He stayed, sealed in place, for the entire hour.

Rahman Bey's most vocal critic was, of course, Houdini. He was familiar with most of the man's stunts from his dime museum days. There was nothing paranormal about them. It was all simply a matter of knowledge and training. Harry could do all of the stunts himself -- except for being buried alive. He had been buried beneath the ground once in California, and he had been locked into boxes and coffins underwater a countless number of times. But his aim had always been to try and free himself as quickly as possible.

In late July, Bey's manager publicly challenged Houdini to duplicate the water endurance feat. His ego made it impossible for him not to accept the challenge. He was sealed into a container the same size as Bey's and was lowered into the Shelton Hotel pool. An hour and a half later, assistants hauled the box from the water and opened it. Tired, but otherwise in good condition, the magician told reporters that there was nothing supernatural about the stunt. The secret, he explained, was to remain calm, move as little as possible, and breathe with short, regular intakes of air.

Hereward Carrington and some of his supporters, who were present at the pool, discounted Houdini's controlled-breathing explanation. They believed, never having attempted the feat themselves, that a trick had been used to supply Harry with oxygen, either a false compartment in the box or a secret flow through the telephone line that had been installed in the coffin as a safety precaution. They were wrong.

Houdini later told his friend and fellow magician, James S. Harto, that he had trained for weeks in water to get his lungs accustomed to breathing very little air. Houdini had always been able to hold his breath for extended periods of time anyway and the stunt simply required him to train a little harder. He told Harto that he merely had to lie on his back and take very shallow breaths. "There is no doubt in my mind, "he said, "that anyone can do it."

Houdini's explanation was validated in 1958 when James "The Amazing" Randi demonstrated on British television his ability to survive under almost the same circumstances. Randi was younger and weighed less than Houdini but the box he used was the same size. He stayed under water in the coffin for two hours and three minutes.

Having been successful with the makeshift iron box, Houdini bought a $2,500 bronze casket -- just like the one that Rahman Bey had used -- and planned to perform the feat as an attraction during his fall tour, much as he had suspended himself in a straitjacket above the city streets in the past. A new lithograph poster was printed to publicize the stunt: "Buried Alive! Egyptian Fakirs Outdone! Master Mystifier Houdini 'The Greatest Necromancer of the Age -- Perhaps of All Time,' his favorite quote from a *Literary Digest* story. The poster depicted a coffin, with a cutaway section that showed Houdini tied up inside, resting against the edge of an Egyptian burial chamber. To the right was the Sphinx and above it, in a swirl of mist, was Harry's face.

Houdini's fall season began in September in Paterson, New Jersey. It would be during this tour that the show began to be plagued with problems and mishaps and soon, the curtain would fall on the great magician for all time.

THE DEATH OF HOUDINI

In October 1926, Houdini began a week-long engagement in Providence, Rhode Island. When Bess awoke sick and feverish one morning, Harry, who never consulted a doctor himself unless Bess cried and threatened to leave him, had a physician at her bedside within the hour. The doctor pronounced ptomaine poisoning as the source of her illness and Harry put in a hurried call to New York to summon a nurse to come and travel with her. On Friday evening, Bess' temperature rose and Houdini sat with her throughout the night.

On Saturday morning, the fever finally broke. Harry managed a few hours of restless sleep between the matinee show and the evening performance. After the last show, Harry saw Bess, her nurse and his troupe off for Albany at the railroad station, then boarded the last train for New York City. He dozed occasionally in his seat, but the stops and starts of the train in various stations kept him awake for most of the journey.

Harry had a meeting with Bernard Ernst when he arrived back in the city but the family maid told him that Ernst had not yet returned from a trip. He was expected anytime and Houdini was welcome to wait. He dozed on a couch in the living room until Ernst returned.

A few hours later, Harry called Albany. The nurse reported that his wife's condition had not changed. He met with Frank Ducrot, who now owned the magic shop that Houdini once managed, to arrange for several pieces of apparatus for his show. He telephoned Albany again and the nurse advised him not to worry; she planned to stay with Bess through the night.

Houdini took the early morning train to Albany, again staying awake most of the trip. Bess was better when he arrived at the hotel but was still not well enough to leave her bed. He managed a brief nap before the opening night performance on October 11. During the show, a chain slipped during Houdini's famous Chinese Water Torture Cell escape and he fractured his ankle. A doctor in the audience advised him to end the show and go to the hospital but he refused. In fact, he finished the entire performance painfully hopping on one foot. Afterwards, he stopped at Memorial Hospital in Albany for treatment and x-rays. He was ordered to stay off his feet for at least one week, but he continued his shows anyway.

The newspapers predicted that Harry's injury would keep him off the stage for some time, but the reporters underestimated his stamina and drive. It would take more than a broken bone to stop a Houdini tour. Harry fashioned a leg support for himself and went on to Schenectady and Montreal.

On October 18, he opened at the Princess Theatre and a doctor examined his ankle. He told him the same thing that the earlier doctor had: stay off it for a week and the bone would knit. Houdini continued to lecture and perform, although he did remain seated during his lectures. After one lecture at McGill University, students and faculty members surged forward to meet him. One young man showed Houdini a sketch he had made while Harry had been talking. The magician pronounced it as an excellent likeness. He autographed the picture and invited the artist to make a close-up portrait later in the week backstage at the theater.

On the afternoon of Friday, October 22, the McGill University artist, Samuel J. Smiley, and Jack Price, a fellow student and friend, met Houdini in the theater lobby around 11:00 a.m. There was a crowd at the ticket window and Harry arrived with Bess, the nurse and a secretary. The nurse suggested that they have lunch and Houdini agreed that it was time to eat. He made a hot dog appear from the hat of a startled female bystander, then escorted the students to his dressing room.

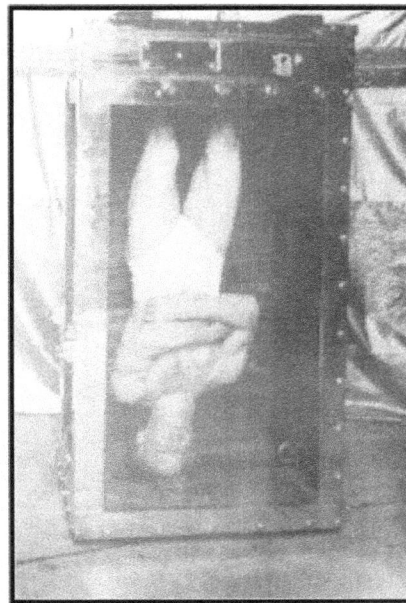

Houdini in the Chinese Torture Cell. A slip when he entered the tank caused an ankle fracture on October 11, 1926. He finished the rest of the show hopping on one foot. Although ordered by a doctor to stay off the foot for at least a week, Harry continued to perform.

Harry hung up his hat and overcoat, took off his jacket, rolled up his sleeves and removed his tie. He opened his shirt collar, and leaned back on the couch to look through a pile of letters on his dressing room table. He was talking about his career as Smiley began to sketch the portrait.

He was hard at work on the drawing when a third student, J. Gordon Whitehead, came in and began talking to the magician. Houdini was very courteous to the young man but was also occupied with his mail. He wasn't paying close attention when Whitehead asked if it was true that Houdini could withstand powerful blows to the stomach. He absently replied that he could as long as he had time to brace himself in anticipation of the punch. The boy, thinking that Houdini had given permission for just such a demonstration, suddenly leaned forward and struck him four times in the abdomen with a clenched fist. When Houdini looked startled, the boy quickly backed away, explaining in a panic that he thought that Houdini had given him

The Garrick Theater in Detroit, Houdini's final venue. On the right is a newspaper ad for what turned out to be Harry's final show.

permission to hit him. Smiley and Price thought Whitehead had gone mad and grabbed for the boy to pull him away. Houdini stopped them with a pained wave. Whitehead felt terrible seeing the performer so clearly in pain, but the magician soon recovered enough to reassure the young man and then step onto the stage for his show.

Throughout the evening, Houdini was seen wincing in pain and late that night, he admitting to crippling pains that continued to get worse. He was unable to sleep when he returned to his hotel room and Bess, believing that he had a stomach cramp or a strained muscle, massaged him in an effort to make him more comfortable.

His performances over the next two days consisted of hours of agony, save for brief intermissions when he fell into a restless sleep. After his final Saturday show, he told his wife about what had happened in the dressing room. By then, it was too late to get a doctor. An assistant wired the show's advance man in Detroit and told him to have a physician ready who could see Houdini when they arrived. The train arrived late and Houdini went straight to the Garrick Theater rather than to the Statler Hotel, where Dr. Leo Dretzka was waiting in the lobby. When the doctor finally got to the theater, he found Houdini busy helping his assistants with props for the evening show. There was no cot in the dressing room where Dr. Dretzka could examine the magician, so Houdini stretched out on the floor. He was diagnosed as having acute appendicitis. He had a fever of 102 degrees but refused to go to the hospital for the emergency surgery that he needed. He was scheduled to perform at a sold-out show that night and was determined to be there. The theater manager had already told him that the house was full. Houdini replied: "They're here to see me. I won't disappoint them."

By the time that he took the stage, his fever had gone up to 104. He was tired, feverish and

Grace Hospital, where Houdini died. At right,, thousands streamed past Houdini's coffin during his funeral.

tormented by abdominal pains, plus he was hobbling on the broken ankle from two weeks earlier. He somehow managed to perform the entire show, although his terrified assistants were constantly forced to complete some motion that Houdini couldn't manage. Spectators reported that he often missed his cues and that he seemed to hurry the show along. Between the first and second acts, he was taken to his dressing room and ice packs were placed on him to try and cool his fever. This was repeated between acts two and three as well. Toward the end of the evening, he began doing what he called "little magic" with silks and coins, card sleights and accepting questions and challenges from the audience. He remained on the stage throughout the evening but just before the third act, he turned to his chief assistant and murmured "Drop the curtain, Collins, I can't go any further." When the curtain closed, he literally collapsed where he had been standing. Houdini was helped back to his dressing room where he changed his clothes but still refused to go back to the hospital.

He went to his hotel, still convinced that his pain and illness would subside. It was not until the early morning hours, when Bess threw a tantrum, that the hotel physician was summoned. He in turn contacted a surgeon and Houdini was rushed to the hospital, against his will. An operation was performed immediately but the surgeons agreed that there was little hope for him to pull through. His appendix had ruptured and despite the efforts of medical experts, it was suggested that Bess contact family members.

Despite the seriousness of his condition, Houdini managed to hang on until the early afternoon of October 31. Finally, he turned to Bess and his brother, Theo, who he affectionately called "Dash," and spoke quietly to them: "Dash, I'm getting tired and I can't fight anymore. I guess this thing is going to get me."

A moment later, Houdini stepped through the curtain between this world and the next.

MYSTERIES OF HOUDINI'S DEATH

Many mysteries still surround the death of Houdini, although many of these mysteries have come about thanks to the fact that there are at least seven different versions of how his death occurred. They include him dying in the arms of Bess in Boston and Chicago, dying while hanging suspended upside-down in a glass tank, dying while performing at the bottom of a river, dying while trapped in a locked casket and others. What actually happened is that Houdini died of a ruptured appendix. It's likely that Houdini was suffering from appendicitis before the young man punched him in the abdomen. The rain of blows could have caused the actual rupture. However, one or more punches is generally accepted as the cause of death.

More mysteries came about in the days following his death as reports from clairvoyants who claimed to have predicted Houdini's death, and to have witnessed signs and omens of it began coming in. A Mr. Gysel stated that at 10:58 on the evening of October 24, a photograph of Houdini that he had framed and hung on the wall suddenly "fell to the ground, breaking the glass. I now know that Houdini will die," he allegedly said.

Gysel's prediction came as no surprise to Houdini's Spiritualist adversaries, who had been predicting his death for years. Sooner or later, they were bound to be correct. In 1924, Margery's spirit guide, Walter, had given him "a year or less" and he was not the only one. According to Sir Arthur Conan Doyle, he and others in his "home circle" had recorded an ominous message about the magician several months before his death. The message read: "Houdini is doomed, doomed, doomed!" And on October 13, a medium named Mrs. Wood wrote a letter to the novelist Fulton Oursler that read: "Three years ago, the spirit of Dr. Hyslop said 'the waters are black for Houdini' and he foretold disaster would claim him while performing before an audience in a theatre. Dr. Hyslop now says the injury is more serious than has been reported and that Houdini's days as a magician are over."

According to some accounts, Houdini himself had premonitions of the coming events. Among his clippings was one from 1919 recording the onstage collapse of a comedian named Sidney

Drew. The performer had taken ill in St. Louis, but had continued to play, against all advice, until in Detroit, when he could simply go no further. Those who discovered this clipping among Houdini's belongings must have found the death of the comedian to be eerily similar to that of Houdini himself. Why the magician saved it is unknown.

His friend and fellow magician, Joseph Dunninger, also had an eerie story to recall after Houdini's death. He said that on one early morning in October 1926, Houdini called him in New York and asked him to come with his car to West 113th Street, as he was in a hurry and had to move some things. When the car was loaded, he asked Dunninger to drive through the park.

Dunninger said that as they got to the exit on Central Park West, around 72nd Street, Houdini grabbed him by the arm and urged him to go back to his house. Puzzled, Dunninger asked him if he had forgot something. "Don't ask questions, Joe," Houdini replied, "just turn around and go back."

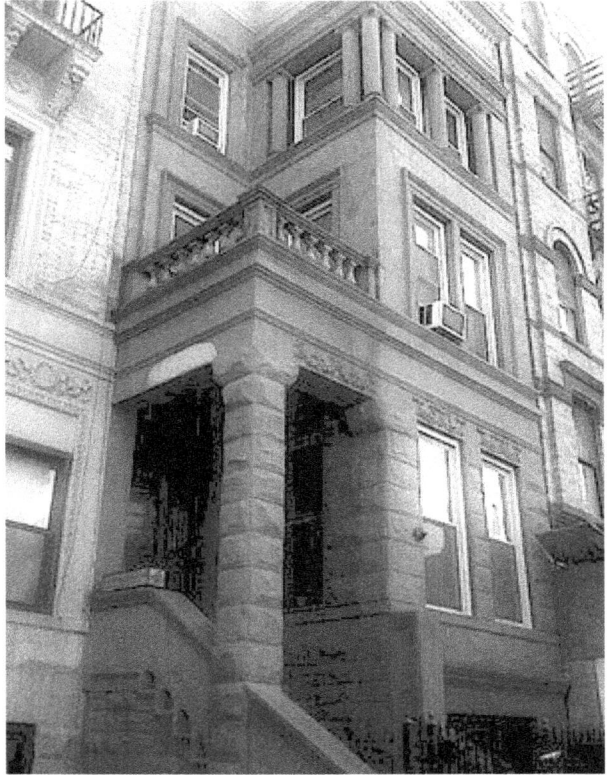

Houdini's house on West 113th Street in New York

Dunninger drove back to the house and when they arrived, Houdini climbed out of the car and stood looking at the brownstone in the rain. He stayed that way, water dripping down his face and soaking his clothing, for a few minutes and then he got back into the car without saying a word. Dunninger drove off and when the two men again approached the western exit of the park, he glanced over and saw that Houdini's shoulders had started to shake. He was crying. His friend asked him what was wrong and Houdini gave a rather cryptic answer: "I've seen my house for the last time, Joe. I'll never see my house again."

"And as far as I know," Dunninger later wrote. "He never did."

THE HOUDINI SEANCES

Not long after Houdini's death, the famous "Houdini Séances" began and not surprisingly, they still continue today, although the official sanction of the Houdini estate ended years ago. While Bess planned to honor her husband's requests about attempting contact with him after death, this may not have been what prompted her to seek the secret code that he promised to send her from beyond the grave, if possible. Like her husband had been at the death of his mother, Bess was at a loss as to what to do with her life with Houdini gone. They had been together since Bess had been a young woman and she had been living inside   his closed world, filling the role as his wife and assistant for decades. She had been his partner in a very real sense and he always stated that Bess was his "beloved wife... and the only one who had ever helped me in my work." Although their life had not been perfect, it had never been dull and as huge as Houdini's ego had been, he never made it a secret that he depended on her totally. With him gone, Bess seemed to be drifting and empty. It's no surprise that she wanted desperately to speak with him again.

But her life moved shakily on. While she was not rich, Houdini had left a trust fund for

Bess and Theo at Harry's grave in Machpelah Cemetery in Queens, New York. The massive monument features a weeping mourner and a bust of Houdini.

her and substantial amounts of life insurance had been carried on him. She had to pay heavy inheritance taxes but she had more than enough to live comfortably for the rest of her life. She sold their house on West 113th Street, moved to Payson Avenue in another part of the city, and became lost in alcohol and misery. She tried opening a tea room and thought of taking a vaudeville act on the road, but none of these projects really got off the ground. She soon began to spend her time attempting to contact her husband. Every Sunday at the hour of his death, she would shut herself in a room with his photograph and wait for a sign. She confirmed that she was waiting for a secret message from her husband and word spread far and wide that Bess had offered $10,000 to any medium who could deliver a true message from Houdini.

Almost weekly, another medium came forward claiming to have broken the code, but none of them did until 1928, when famed medium Arthur Ford announced that he had a message for Bess. He told her that the message had come from Houdini's mother and consisted of

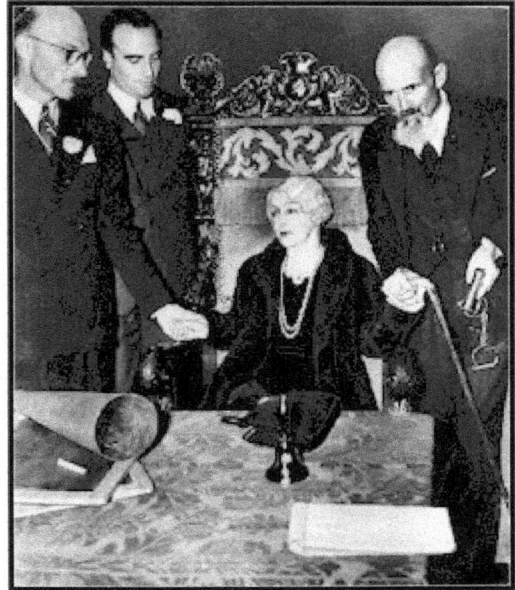

Bess began the "Houdini Seances" shortly after her husband's death. They were held frequently in the beginning and then eventually, became an annual event on October 31, the day Harry died.

a single word, which was "forgive." With this, Bess had a startling announcement to make --- claiming that Ford's message was the first that she had received which "had any appearance of the truth."

It was the one word that Houdini had always hoped to hear from his mother in the séance room. It had to do with an incident that happened many years before. When his brother Nat's wife, Sadie, had abandoned him to marry another brother, Leopold, Houdini had been shocked and angry. The once close-knit harmony of the Weiss family had been destroyed. Harry could not bring himself to forgive his brother unless his mother told him to. She died before he could discuss the family crisis with her. This was the one reason that he had searched so tirelessly for a genuine medium and was so infuriated when he found nothing but fakes.

In November, another message came to Ford, this time from Houdini himself. In a trance, the medium relayed an entire coded message: "Rosabelle, answer, tell, pray, answer, look, tell, answer, answer, tell."

After this information was relayed to Bess, she invited Ford to her home and he asked her if the words were correct. She said they were and Ford asked her to remove her wedding ring and tell everyone present what "Rosabelle" meant. This was the word that made the message authentic, a secret known only to Bess and Harry themselves. It was the title of a song that had

Arthur Ford -- the man who claimed to break the Houdini code. He offered the only legitimate response to the secret phrase left by Bess and Harry. But did he obtain it by ethical means?

been popular at Coney Island when they first met. The rest of the message was a series of code words that spelled out the word "believe." The code was one that the Houdinis had used during the "mind-reading act" they perfected in their early days touring with the circus.

This seemed to make the message authentic and appeared to be the final clue that Houdini had promised to relay from the next world. But did Houdini actually communicate from the other side?

Not surprisingly, there were soon accusations of fraud leveled against Arthur Ford. Even though Bess claimed the message was correct, many claimed that Ford had gotten the code from a book about Houdini published in 1927. The press, the skeptics and Houdini's friends refused to accept that Ford had broken the code and Bess, on their advice, withdrew her reward offer.

So, did he really break the "impossible" code? Arthur Ford certainly maintained that he had, going to his grave in 1974 with the firm belief that he had actually received a message from Houdini. In 1928, Ford had been the pastor of the First Spiritualist Church of Manhattan and was a respected member of the psychic community. He had also recently distinguished himself by challenging the magician Howard Thurston to a debate at Carnegie Hall, which Ford won.

Thurston, who had been carrying on Houdini's tradition of exposing fraudulent mediums, was stymied by being unable to explain some of the effects that Ford produced. After he came forward with the code, jealous colleagues turned on Ford and newspaper reporters and debunkers began to charge him with perpetrating a hoax, along with Bess, despite their claims of innocence. Shortly afterwards, Ford was expelled from the United Spiritualist League of New York but was later reinstated "on the grounds of insufficient evidence."

But was he a fraud? Many people believe so and state that he actually found the "secret" code on page 105 of a book that was published the year before. Incidentally, the code was not one that was specially prepared by Houdini and Bess. It was very old and had been used in their act even though it had been around for years. Despite all of this however, it should be noted that while Ford could have easily found the code somewhere --- there has never been an adequate explanation (outside of a fraud perpetrated with Mrs. Houdini, which was denied by both parties) as to where he got the message that he gave to Bess.

Could it have come from the other side?

Bess Houdini continued to hold séances in hopes of communicating with her late husband but as the years went by, she began to lose hope that she would ever hear from him. The last "official" Houdini séance was held on Halloween night in 1936, ten years after Houdini had died. A group of friends, fellow magicians, occultists, scientists and Bess Houdini herself gathered in Hollywood, on the roof of the Knickerbocker Hotel. Eddy Saint, a former carnival and vaudeville showman who had also worked as a magician had arranged the

Eddie Saint, Bess Houdini and Theo Weiss in 1936 at the time of the last Official Houdini Seance

gathering. He had been recommended to Bess a few years before in New York to act as her manager, although concerned friends had actually hired him to watch over her and to protect her from being taken advantage of. A genuine affection developed between then and eventually they began sharing a bungalow together in Hollywood, a place where Bess had enjoyed living during her husband's brief movie career.

Radio coverage for the Final Houdini Séance was provided and it was broadcast all over the world. Eddy Saint took charge of the proceedings and started things off with the playing of "Pomp and Circumstance," a tune that had been used by Houdini to start his act in the later years. He noted for the radio listeners: "Every facility has been provided tonight that might aid in opening the pathway to the spirit world. Here in the inner circle reposes a "medium's trumpet," a pair of slates with chalk, a writing tablet and pencil, a small bell and in the center reposes a huge pair of silver handcuffs on a silk cushion."

Saint continued coverage of the event, finally crying out to make contact with the late magician: "Houdini! Are you here? Are you here, Houdini? Please manifest yourself in any way possible... We have waited, Houdini, oh so long! Never have you been able to present the evidence you promised. And now, this, the night of nights... the world is listening, Harry... Levitate the table! Move it! Lift the table! Move it or rap it! Spell out a code, Harry... please! Ring a bell! Let its tinkle be heard around the world!"

Saint and the rest of Bess' inner circle attempted to contact the elusive magician for over an hour before finally giving up. Saint finally turned to Bess: "Mrs. Houdini, the zero hour has passed. The ten years are up. Have you reached a decision?"

The mournful voice of Bess Houdini then echoed through radio receivers around the world. "Yes, Houdini did not come through," she replied. "My last hope is gone. I do not believe that Houdini can come back to me --- or to anyone. The Houdini shrine has burned for ten years. I now, reverently... turn out the light. It is finished. Good night, Harry!"

The séance came to an end, but at the moment it did, a tremendously violent thunderstorm broke out, drenching the séance participants and terrifying them with horrific lightning and thunder. They would later learn that this mysterious storm did not occur anywhere else in Hollywood --- only above the Knickerbocker Hotel! Some speculated that perhaps Houdini did come through after all, as the flamboyant performer just might have made his presence known by the spectacular effects of the thunderstorm.

Legends or lies? Who can really say? Houdini was (and remains) a riddle. On one hand, he was an open-minded seeker of truth but on the other, he was a steadfast disbeliever in all things supernatural. If it can be said that a man is gone, but never forgotten, this should be said about Harry Houdini. He is truly, like Spiritualism itself, an American enigma!

BIBLIOGRAPHY AND RECOMMEND READING

Bell, Dan - *The Man Who Killed Houdini* (2004)
Bird, J. Malcolm - *Margery, the Medium* (1925)
Blum, Deborah - *Ghost Hunters* (2006)
Brandon, Ruth - *Life and Many Deaths of Harry Houdini* (1993)
Brandon, Ruth - *The Spiritualists* (1983)
Brown, Slater - *The Heyday of Spiritualism* (1970)
Cannell, J.C. - *Secrets of Houdini* (1932)
Christopher, Melbourne - *Houdini: The Untold Story* (1969)
        "   - *Houdini: A Pictorial Life* (1976)
Christopher, Milbourne & Maurine - *Illustrated History of Magic* (1976)
Clarke, Robert (Publisher) *Spirits & Spirit Worlds* (1975)
Doyle, Sir Arthur Conan Doyle - *History of Spiritualism* (1926)
        "   - *Memories and Adventures* (1924)
        "   - *The Edge of the Unknown* (1930)
Dunninger, Joseph - *Houdini's Spirit Exposes* (1928)
        "   - *Magic & Mystery* (1967)
Ernst, Bernard & Hereward Carrington - *Houdini & Conan Doyle: The Story of a Strange Friendship* (1933)
Ford, Arthur - *Nothing so Strange* (1958)
Gibson, Walter - *Houdini's Escapes* (1930)
        "   - *Houdini's Magic* (1932)
        "   - *The Master Magicians* (1966)
        "   *Secrets of Magic* (1967)
Gresham, William Lindsay - *Houdini: The Man Who Walked Through Walls* (1959)
Guiley, Rosemary Ellen - *Encyclopedia of Ghosts and Spirits* (1992 / 2000)
Haining, Peter - *Ghosts: The Illustrated History* (1987)
Hall, Trevor - *The Spiritualists* (1962)
Houdini, Harry - *Handcuff Secrets* (1907)

"   - *Houdini's Paper Magic* (1921)
"   - *Magical Rope Ties and Escapes* (1920)
"   - *Magician Among the Spirits* (1924)
"   - *Miracle Mongers and their Methods* (1920)
"   - *The Right Way to Do Wrong* (1906)
"   - *The Unmasking of Robert Houdin* (1908)
Kalush, William & Larry Sloman - *The Secret Life of Houdini* (2006)
Kendall, Lace - *Houdini, Master of Escape* (1960)
McHargue, Georgess - *Facts, Frauds and Phantasms* (1972)
Miller, R. DeWitt - *Impossible, Yet it Happened* (1947)
Mose, Arthur - *Houdini Speaks Out!* (2007)
Pearsall, Ronald - *The Table Rappers* (1972)
Permutt, Cyril - *Photographing the Spirit World* (1983)
Picknett, Lynn - *Flights of Fancy* (1987)
Reader's Digest Books - *Into the Unknown* (1981)
Somerlott, Robert - *Here, Mr. Splitfoot* (1971)
Silverman, Kenneth - *Houdini!* (1996)
Spraggett, Allen - *Arthur Ford: Man who Talked with the Dead* (1973)
Stashower, Daniel - *Teller of Tales: Life of Sir Arthur Conan Doyle* (1999)
Steinmeyer, Jim - *Hiding the Elephant* (2003)
Taylor, Troy - *Ghosts by Gaslight* (2007)
"   - *The Ghost Hunter's Guidebook* (1999 / 2001)
"   - *Sex & the Supernatural* (2009)

Magazines & Periodicals:

American History / August 1999: The Medium & The Magician (Daniel Stashower)
Fate / March 1960: Margery was a Fraud (Alson Smith)
Fate / September 1961: When Congress Investigated Spiritualism (Richard Saunders)
Fate / August 1963: Mystery of Houdini's Death (Vincent Gaddis)
Fate / November 1971: Arthur Ford Goes a Round with the Magicians (Arthur Ford)
Fate / April 1985: Margery Mediumship (Marian Nester)

Special Thanks to:
Jill Hand -- Editor
Mike Schwab - Cover Design
Rene Kruse
John Winterbauer
Ken Berg
Crusty & Houseshoe
And Haven Taylor

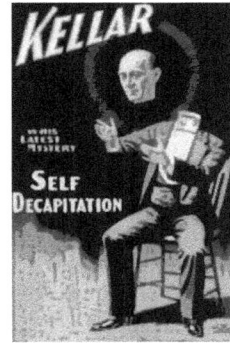

ABOUT THE AUTHOR

Troy Taylor is an occultist, crime buff, supernatural historian and the author of nearly 70 books on ghosts, hauntings, history, crime and the unexplained in America.

He is also the founder of the American Ghost Society and the owner of the American Hauntings Tour company.

Taylor shares a birthday with one of his favorite authors, F. Scott Fitzgerald, but instead of living in New York and Paris like Fitzgerald, Taylor grew up in Illinois. Raised on the prairies of the state, he developed an interest in "things that go bump in the night" at an early age and as a young man, began developing ghost tours and writing about hauntings and crime in Chicago and Central Illinois. His writings have now taken him all over the country and into some of the most far-flung corners of the world.

He began his first book in 1989, which delved into the history and hauntings of his hometown of Decatur, Illinois, and in 1994, it spawned the Haunted Decatur Tour -- and eventually led to the founding of his Illinois Hauntings Tours (with current tours in Alton, Chicago, Decatur, Lebanon & Jacksonville) and the American Hauntings Tours, which travel all over the country in search of haunted places.

Along with writing about the unusual and hosting tours, Taylor has also presented on the subjects of ghosts, hauntings and crime for public and private groups. He has also appeared in scores of newspaper and magazine articles about these subjects and in hundreds of radio and television broadcasts about the supernatural. Taylor has appeared in a number of documentary films, several television series and in one feature film about the paranormal.

Troy and his wife, Haven -- when they are not traveling -- currently reside in Chicago.

WHITECHAPEL PRESS

Whitechapel Productions Press is a division of Dark Haven Entertainment and a small press publisher, specializing in books about ghosts and hauntings. Since 1993, the company has been one of America's leading publishers of supernatural books and has produced such best-selling titles as *Haunted Illinois, The Ghost Hunter's Guidebook, Ghosts on Film, Confessions of a Ghost Hunter, The Haunting of America, Sex & the Supernatural* the *Dead Men Do Tell Tales* crime series and many others.

With more than a dozen different authors producing high quality books on all aspects of ghosts, hauntings and the paranormal, Whitechapel Press has made its mark with America's ghost enthusiasts.

You can visit Whitechapel Productions Press online and browse through our selection of ghostly titles, plus get information on ghosts and hauntings, haunted history, spirit photographs, information on ghost hunting and much more. by visiting the internet website at:

WWW.AMERICAN HAUNTINGS.ORG

AMERICAN HAUNTINGS TOURS

Founded in 1994 by author Troy Taylor, the American Hauntings Tour Company (which includes the Illinois Hauntings Tours) is America's oldest and most experienced tour company that takes ghost enthusiasts around the country for excursions and overnight stays at some of America's most haunted places.

In addition to our tours of America's haunted places, we also offer tours of Illinois' most haunted cities, including Chicago, Alton, Decatur, Lebanon and Jacksonville. These award-winning ghost tours run all year around, with seasonal tours only in some cities.

Find out more about tours, and make reservations online, by visiting the internet website at:

WWW.AMERICAN HAUNTINGS.ORG

www.ingramcontent.com/pod-product-compliance
Lightning Source LLC
Chambersburg PA
CBHW081152090426
42736CB00017B/3281